"This book surprised me—in a deli[...] me understand our eternal home. It certainly does [...] *Remember Heaven* connects this world and this life to the future. It fuels daily living by considering everlasting life. It renews hope by exploring how heaven relates to earth. This book is not just about heaven but also about recovering hope in everyday life. Read this book and get ready for some heaven-sent encouragement."

Mark Vroegop, President, The Gospel Coalition; author, *Dark Clouds, Deep Mercy*

"This book is beautifully written and profoundly reorienting. Matt McCullough deftly shows us the deep consolation and bright hope we have in Christ. I hadn't realized how much I needed it."

Sam Allberry, Associate Pastor, Immanuel Nashville, Tennessee; author, *One with My Lord*

"I know few authors who can approach Matt McCullough's ability to write with pastoral sensitivity, biblical insight, and cultural awareness. This book will challenge and encourage you with the hope of heaven, the 'rebirthright' of every Christian. Don't settle for the dismal distractions of this world."

Collin Hansen, Vice President for Content and Editor in Chief, The Gospel Coalition; Host, *Gospelbound* podcast

"In a world distracted by temporary pleasures, even Christians can lose sight of the wonders of heaven. Matt McCullough reminds us that where we place our hope matters, as he skillfully redirects our focus to the sure and glorious future God has promised. Chapter by chapter, this book provides profoundly practical insights for living faithfully in the here and now, all through the lens of the eternal joy that awaits us."

Jenny Manley, author, *The Good Portion—Christ: Delighting in the Doctrine of Christ*

"Matt McCullough is a delight to read. *Remember Death* blew me away a few years ago. Sure enough, *Remember Heaven* is masterful too. Matt has an uncommon ability to apply soaring truth to everyday life, with surgical precision and pastoral care. Turning these pages moved me to long for the world to come and, ultimately, for the King who is coming. And it reinvigorated me to think and live differently now. Cheer up, brothers and sisters! Our future is unimaginably bright."

Matt Smethurst, Lead Pastor, River City Baptist Church, Richmond, Virginia; author, *Tim Keller on the Christian Life* and *Before You Share Your Faith*; Cohost, *The Everyday Pastor* podcast

"In *Remember Heaven*, Matt McCullough probes several of our most common struggles, with sensitivity and insight, and he shows how each facet of the hope of heaven can nourish and sustain us. I love this book. I needed this book. I'm pretty confident that you need this book too. I highly recommend it and plan to give away lots of copies."

Bobby Jamieson, Senior Pastor, Trinity Baptist Church, Chapel Hill, North Carolina; author, *Everything Is Never Enough: Ecclesiastes' Surprising Path to Resilient Happiness*

Remember Heaven

Remember Heaven

*Meditations on the World to Come
for Life in the Meantime*

Matthew McCullough

CROSSWAY®

WHEATON, ILLINOIS

Remember Heaven: Meditations on the World to Come for Life in the Meantime

© 2025 by Matthew McCullough

Published by Crossway
          1300 Crescent Street
          Wheaton, Illinois 60187

Cover design: David Fassett

First printing 2025

Printed in the United States of America

Trade paperback ISBN: 978-1-4335-9916-3
ePub ISBN: 978-1-4335-9918-7
PDF ISBN: 978-1-4335-9917-0

Library of Congress Cataloging-in-Publication Data

Names: McCullough, Matthew, author.

Title: Remember heaven : meditations on the world to come for life in the meantime / Matthew McCullough.

Description: Wheaton, Illinois : Crossway, 2025. | Series: The gospel coalition | Includes bibliographical references and index.

Identifiers: LCCN 2024035216 (print) | LCCN 2024035217 (ebook) | ISBN 9781433599163 (trade paperback) | ISBN 9781433599170 (pdf) | ISBN 9781433599187 (epub)

Subjects: LCSH: Future life. | Heaven. | Christian life.

Classification: LCC BT903 .M446 2025 (print) | LCC BT903 (ebook) | DDC 248.4—dc23/eng/20241113

LC record available at https://lccn.loc.gov/2024035216

LC ebook record available at https://lccn.loc.gov/2024035217

Crossway is a publishing ministry of Good News Publishers.

VP			33	32	31	30	29	28	27	26	25
14	13	12	11	10	9	8	7	6	5	4	3	2	1

For my father, Mark,
who has
gladly chosen tents in this world,
firmly set his eyes on the city to come,
and
faithfully shown me what he sees.

Contents

Acknowledgments

THANK YOU, Edgefield Church family, for the unspeakable joy of being your pastor and for doing so much to prepare me for the world to come. I love you guys. And I'm more grateful than ever to be walking home with all of you.

To my fellow elders at Edgefield, thank you for encouraging me to write and for all the structural support that makes it possible. I don't deserve the privilege of serving with each of you. But, my goodness, am I glad I get to.

I'm grateful to Ivan Mesa, Collin Hansen, and the Gospel Coalition editorial team who saw potential in this idea and guided me every step of the way. What a gift to have friends who get such evident joy from helping others say what they have to say. Thank you, too, to the amazing team at Crossway, especially Todd Augustine and Gerard Cruz. It's an amazing privilege to work with a publisher whose books have meant so much to me over the years.

Whatever flaws remain in these pages, I can promise you there would be far more if not for the many friends who gave me feedback on drafts along the way: Lynn Henderson, Seth Jones, Rama Kumaran, Bill Heerman, Joshua Minchin, Stephanie Mitchell,

Carly Prentice, and Emily Riley. Thank you for your time, for your insight, and for the love that shared them with me.

Lindsey—I have no sweeter foretaste of the marriage feast to come than the everyday joy of our marriage in the meantime. I love you.

Walter, Sam, and Benjamin—I'm sure no father has ever had more fun than I have had being your dad. More than anything, I want this joy to last forever. Through Jesus it can.

And finally, I thank my parents, Mark and Amy, who were the first to show me the beauty of Jesus and who have made it so clear throughout my life that they are seeking a homeland. "But as it is, they desire a better country, that is, a heavenly one. Therefore God is not ashamed to be called their God, for he has prepared for them a city" (Heb. 11:16). Happy seventieth birthday, Dad.

Introduction

Set Your Mind

*How the Hope of Heaven Grounds
Our Lives as Christians*

ANOTHER CHRISTMAS just came and went, along with a wonderful week away with our extended family.

We had been counting down the days to that trip from the time we finished our Halloween candy. We knew it meant a break from the grind of normal life. We knew we'd see grandparents, aunts, uncles, and cousins we only see a couple of times each year. We knew the favorite foods we'd be eating and that there would be presents. Our trip was packed with all this goodness and more.

Just a few days after returning, I could already feel it. The dreaded postholiday blues. Do you know what I'm talking about? I haven't seen any scientific data to back this up, but I've seen enough life to know that this phenomenon is real. And it has two important lessons to teach us.

First, it is incredible what a difference it makes when you have something to look forward to. An exciting event on your horizon can change how you see everything else in your life. Adults are less bothered by annoying problems at work. Kids are less likely to bicker with siblings around the house. Even those facing terminal illness can draw inspiration and even some relief by thinking ahead to another Christmas with the people they love most. It's simply wonderful to have something to look forward to.

The second lesson is more sobering. What we really need is something to look forward to that won't leave us back where we began. This Christmas I got a sharp-looking, quarter-zip pullover sweater. I expect to be wearing it for the next decade or more, long after it's gone out of style. But I know it will eventually wear out. Even more to the point, it doesn't change anything about what I see when I look in the mirror. It can't remove the not-so-hidden, middle-age paunch underneath. It can't put a single hair back on my bald head. It hasn't plucked the gray out of my whiskers. As for work, the stress I left behind was still stressing me out when I got back. My holiday was truly wonderful. I was right to look forward to it. But nothing I enjoyed about it lasted for more than a week, and I ended up right back where I started.

Hope matters. We can't live without it. But what we hope *in* matters even more. We need a hope strong enough to bear the weight of our lives in the meantime. And that is precisely what we have in the hope of heaven.

What is the hope of heaven to your life as a Christian? That is the simple question I want to raise and help you answer through this book. The question flows from Paul's words at the beginning of what may be his most beautiful and comprehensive passage on living as a follower of Jesus:

> If then you have been raised with Christ, seek the things that
> are above, where Christ is, seated at the right hand of God. Set

your minds on things that are above, not on things that are on earth. For you have died, and your life is hidden with Christ in God. When Christ who is your life appears, then you also will appear with him in glory. (Col. 3:1–4)

In Colossians 3 Paul talks about envy, idolatry, anger, and slander. He talks about kindness, compassion, patience, and forgiveness. He talks about sex, marriage, and parenting. Yet every bit of this portrait—from what sins to put off to what virtues to put on, from how we love one another to how we conduct ourselves in church and at home and in the workplace—flows from a mind that is set on things above.

Right at the center of the Christian life, Paul places an intentional, disciplined, cultivated focus on heaven. Does that sound right to you?

I'm convinced that heaven suffers from a serious brand problem.

For some, the idea of heaven seems boring. This is a problem with a long pedigree. Catherine Earnshaw, of Emily Brontë's *Wuthering Heights*, speaks from nineteenth-century England what many people feel today:

> If I were in heaven, Nelly, I should be extremely miserable. . . . I dreamt, once, that I was there. . . . Heaven did not seem to be my home; and I broke my heart with weeping to come back to earth; and the angels were so angry that they flung me out, into the middle of the heath on the top of Wuthering Heights, where I woke sobbing for joy.[1]

Do you see the implication? Heaven is literally a nightmare. As one writer sums it up, "Our ancestors were afraid of hell; we are

---

1 Emily Brontë, *Wuthering Heights* (New York: The Library Paperback Edition, 2000), 99–100.

afraid of heaven. We think it will be boring."[2] Many Christians may know better than to accept clichés about chubby angels playing harps in the clouds, but they don't have more relatable images to fall back on. *Why should I want to be at a worship service that never ends?*

For others, the thought of longing for heaven feels a little bit wrong, as if there's a zero-sum relationship between longing for heaven and loving the world as we know it now, with its precious people and their serious problems. "Heavenly-minded" is an age-old knock on people who are no earthly good. Karl Marx famously described religion as the opiate of the people, something to take the edge off their pain and keep them from taking action to make things better. I've heard Christians of my generation speak of heavenly-mindedness in pretty much those terms, as cover for indifference and inaction. *Isn't it self-indulgent to look ahead to an eternal world of bliss when real people are really suffering all around you?*

For still others, the notion of heaven seems almost pitiful, more like loss than gain—as if heaven means the end of familiar joys in this world, joys that are significant and wonderful. *Why should I long to be in some other world when I've got so much to live for in this world?*

My sense, however, is many Christians simply aren't thinking about heaven at all and, if asked, couldn't say why they should be. Maybe it makes sense why an eighty-three-year-old widow with terminal cancer might long for heaven. But what about a twenty-three-year-old law student in her second year? What about a thirty-three-year-old engineer with his first kid on the way?

---

2 Carol Zaleski, "In Defense of Immortality," *First Things*, August 2000, https://www.first things.com/.

Throughout this book, I want to show that the issue is not whether you *love* this world and its joys, its people and their needs. The question is whether you have any *hope* beyond this world and what it has to offer. Concrete, unshakable, life-giving hope is the birthright of every Christian, and this hope is meant to touch every part of our lives in the meantime.

Sadly, I'm convinced that we tend to view heaven the way we view our car insurance. We know we need to have it, but God forbid we ever have to use it. The best thing about having car insurance is the peace of mind it provides: you don't have to think about it until the moment you need it. Meanwhile your focus stays fixed on the car itself—what style you like best, what features you need, how you want to use it, where you want to drive it.

As the Bible describes heaven, it's not at all like an insurance policy filed and forgotten. It is an inheritance you are sure to receive and, beyond that, an inheritance you can draw on right now. Throughout Scripture, the promise of heaven functions like a trust fund—certain, fully funded, and freely accessible while we wait for faith to turn to sight. I want to help you see the incredible riches stored away in that trust fund and how to draw on that wealth day by day.

But first, back to Paul and his crystal-clear, countercultural basis for our lives as Christians. Why should we set our minds on things above? Why does Paul lay this command as the foundation of the Christian life? I see three reasons, and these frame everything that follows in this book.

Hope Is Essential

Heavenly-mindedness is absolutely vital because what we want or expect from our future has a huge effect on our experience in the meantime. We humans are future-oriented creatures whether we like it or not.

We are not the only creatures with an eye on what's coming, of course. Birds build nests in the springtime. Squirrels bury nuts in the fall. Bears store up fat for winter hibernation. But birds, squirrels, and bears operate on instinct, aimed at simple survival.

Humans alone have hopes and dreams. We imagine opportunities to crave and possibilities to fear. We train for careers. We plan for families. We save for retirement. We buy insurance for our houses, our cars, our health, and even our lives. Only humans make conscious choices now in the hope or dread of what might be later.

The question is not whether your view of the future shapes your life today. The question is which view of the future is shaping your life today and what effect it is having.

Tim Keller often used a helpful thought experiment to capture this point.[3] Imagine two women hired to do the same job, under the same conditions, and for the same amount of time. They both have to perform the same menial tasks, hour after hour, day after day. They both carry on through the same sweltering heat in summer and the same freezing cold in winter. But one of these women was told she would receive $30,000 at the end of the year, while the other woman was promised $30 million.

Surely the one promised $30,000 would struggle to keep going. She would deal with bitterness. Maybe she would feel underappreciated and misused. She'd be looking over her shoulder for other opportunities that might pay more or cost less. She'd be

---

3   Timothy Keller, *Making Sense of God: An Invitation to the Skeptical* (New York: Viking, 2016), 153.

discouraged where she was and afraid of missing out on better options.

But the one promised $30 million would put up with just about anything. She would work day in and day out with a smile on her face because every minute of every day would bring her closer to a payday she couldn't get anywhere else.

What view of your future has functional control over your present? Your mind is set on something still to come. Everything in your Christian life flows from whether that something is the future God has promised to you.

The stakes could not be higher. To face up to life in this world as it is, you need a hope beyond this world that can survive anything. That's because anything can happen. Some of our dreams will fade away. Our bodies will wither and fall. Our relationships will be strained by sin and ultimately lost to death. And more often than not, we can't stay out of our own way as we stumble on toward the grave and what comes next.

Life can be brutal. If you live long enough, in one way or another, it will be. When Jesus said to lay up treasures in heaven, this fundamental truth about the world was his backdrop—this is a world where moths devour, thieves steal, and rust destroys (Matt. 6:19–20). There is a baseline of brokenness to life under death that no one escapes. The only way to face up to this reality is with a hope beyond the reach of death and all its minions—loss, separation, change, time itself. You need a clear view of where all this is going, to carry on no matter what along the way.

Diversion Is Easier

We are commanded to set our minds on things above because it would be so much easier not to. Diversion by one thing or another comes much more naturally. I don't have to tell my kids to finish their ice cream. I do have to command them to take five bites of their cauliflower soup.

Focusing on heaven is more like eating cruciferous vegetables than eating ice cream. It's better for us. It's more nourishing. It builds our strength and our resistance to all sorts of infection. But it is sometimes less attractive than other options competing for our attention and our affection. Apart from the work of God's Spirit in us, the affections of our hearts and the allure of our environment will constantly set our minds on things on earth.

We are relentlessly biased toward false hopes we can see, touch, and control—hopes that can't satisfy us, can't save us, and can't possibly outlive us. This was the story of Adam and Eve in the garden. It was the story of Israel wandering through the wilderness. It was the story of Israel forced into exile. And it is our story too. How do you stay focused on what is unseen and eternal when what is seen and temporary is so present and so powerful?

This is the driving concern behind one of the most important books on heaven ever written: Richard Baxter's *The Saints' Everlasting Rest*. Baxter was a pastor in seventeenth-century England during the bloody years of the English Civil War. Surrounded by that carnage and following a near-death experience of his own, he worked out a process for meditating on heaven as a spiritual discipline.

Baxter was stunned by how little his flock seemed to care about the life to come, despite the obvious difficulty of their lives here and now. The problem as he saw it was not that Christians denied that there is such a place as heaven or even doubted that they themselves might be there someday. The problem was the gap between the head and the heart: "When truth is apprehended only as truth, this is but an unsavory and loose apprehension; when it is apprehended as *good* as well as *true*, this is a solid and delightful apprehending."[4]

In other words, we need a sense of heaven's goodness in the heart before the truth we profess shapes the lives we're living. By nature we have no trouble seeing what's good about power, sex, fame, or money (and what it can buy). But it takes discipline to see the goodness in what is not yet seen—to see God's promise for our future as *good* as well as *true*.

Meditating on heaven, Baxter argues, is how we use our understanding to warm our affections. It throws open "the door between the head and the heart." The meditation he seeks to model is "simply reading over and repeating God's reasons to our hearts and so disputing with ourselves on his argument and terms."[5] It involves using our judgment to compare the allure of the world to the promises of heaven, until the scale tips toward the latter from the former.

This is the work I hope to do chapter by chapter throughout this book. This is not so much a how-to guide as it is an attempt to practice meditating on heaven with you. My goal is to do for the friends that I pastor now in the twenty-first century something like what Baxter did in the seventeenth century for his readers.

However, we face barriers to meditating on heaven that Baxter could not have imagined four hundred years ago.

We Are More Insulated from Death

For one thing, our lives on average are far more insulated from misery than the average Englishman in 1650, with far more

---

4 Richard Baxter, *The Saints' Everlasting Rest*, updated and abridged by Tim Cooper (Wheaton, IL: Crossway, 2022), 120–21. Emphasis mine.

5 Baxter, *Saints' Everlasting Rest*, 130.

opportunities for wealth and comfort. Beginning in the late eighteenth century and accelerating ever since, life expectancy, net worth, and quality of life have skyrocketed throughout the West. I'm not complaining. I wouldn't trade places with anyone from the seventeenth century. But our unprecedented prosperity can radically distort our perspective on this world.

In Baxter's time, death lurked beneath every sniffle. Life expectancy was roughly thirty-five years. Now it is more than twice that number. Modern medicines, skillful doctors, and remarkable technologies make it seem like there's always something more to be done, some other way to push back death to another day.

In Baxter's time, most people died at home, in the same few square feet in which their families spent their lives. They walked to church through the graves of people who were dear to them. The ever-present reality of death gave ever-present incentive to look up and beyond the shadows of life on earth. Now when someone does come to die, more often than not, it's in a sanitized industrial facility, completely isolated from where we live our lives. It's become easier and easier to live most of life as if death is someone else's problem. And without an urgent awareness that life is just a breath, it makes sense that we would set our minds on squeezing as much as possible from this world here and now.

We Are More Secular

Compared to Baxter's time and place, we live in what some philosophers have called a "secular age."[6] I don't mean that we all deny

---

6 The phrase is widely used but most associated with Charles Taylor and his book, *A Secular Age* (Cambridge, MA: Belknap Press of Harvard University Press, 2007). I was introduced to Taylor's work through Jamie Smith's wonderful guide, *How (Not) to Be Secular: Reading Charles Taylor* (Grand Rapids, MI: Eerdmans, 2014).

the existence of God. I mean that in our day-to-day lives, we don't have to assume his existence the same way they did back then. We don't feel as vulnerable to forces beyond our control or recognize our radical dependence on a reality beyond ourselves.

We live our lives surrounded by stunning human achievements, from high-rise buildings to space-traveling rockets to artificial intelligence we created to outpace our own. Our lives are mediated through all sorts of technologies that filter our work and our play and even our relationships. And compared to Baxter's preindustrial world, we enjoy an unimaginable degree of control aimed directly at our own pleasure and comfort. If I want to, I can have blueberries delivered to my door with a couple of hours' notice in the middle of February.

In a world like ours, even Christians can easily lose sight of the fact that every meal, just like every breath, comes from above. It takes effort to remember that we are wholly dependent on God, we answer to God for these lives he's given us, and therefore we ought to look to him in everything.

We Are More Distracted

Perhaps no barrier to heavenly-mindedness is more influential day-to-day or more typical of our modern context than the smartphones we carry around in our pockets, lay on our desks while we're working, then plug in by our pillows while we're sleeping. I recently saw a cartoon from the *New Yorker* featuring a headstone with the image of a smartphone etched near the top. The epitaph had just two lines:

50% LOOKING AT PHONE

50% LOOKING FOR PHONE[7]

---

7 Roz Chast, *New Yorker*, March 18, 2024, https://www.newyorker.com/.

By some estimates adults are spending on average as many as four to six hours per day scrolling on their phones. When you consider how much of that usage happens in spurts, spread out here and there in the middle of whatever else we're supposed to be doing, we're spending all our waking moments drawn to our phones. That makes it tough to set our minds on anything at all, much less on things above and things to come.

How we spend our moments is how we spend our lives. Do you want your life measured by how many fantasy football titles you won? Or how many limited-time deals you grabbed? Or how many likes you got on that family photo? Or how many days in a row you nailed the Wordle challenge?

John Stott once preached to a crowd full of eager young students who were interested in giving their lives to international missions. He reminded them to remember who they were, as citizens of heaven and pilgrims on earth, and to be wary of how quickly we can fix our eyes here below:

> I read some years ago of a young man who found a five-dollar bill on the street and who "from that time on never lifted his eyes when walking. In the course of years he accumulated 29,516 buttons, 54,172 pins, 12 cents, a bent back and a miserly disposition." *But think what he lost.* He couldn't see the radiance of the sunlight, the sheen of the stars, the smile on the face of his friends, or the blossoms of springtime, for his eyes were in the gutter. There are too many Christians like that. We have important duties on earth, but we must never allow them to preoccupy us in such a way that we forget who we are or where we are going.[8]

---

8   John Stott, "The Christian Church Is a Missionary Church," in *Declare His Glory among the Nations*, ed. David M. Howard (Downers Grove, IL: InterVarsity Press, 1977), 90. Emphasis mine.

I'm sure it has never been more difficult to set our minds on things above than it is right now. But the stakes are as high as ever. We have much to lose if we do not and so much to gain if we do. Which brings me to the final reason for Paul's command, and the ultimate motivation for everything that follows in this book.

Christ Is Worthy

In Colossians 3 Paul's ultimate reason for the command that he puts at the foundation of the Christian life is that heaven is where Christ is and where you will be with him someday: "Seek the things that are above, *where Christ is*. . . . When Christ who is your life appears, then you also will appear with him in glory" (3:1, 4).

It is really hard to feel a vested interest in a place you've never visited before. I live for annual vacations in the Appalachian Mountains because I've traveled there at least once a year for most of my life. When the time for one of those trips gets closer, I have trouble thinking about anything else. I know from experience exactly what it's like to hike those trails, take in those mountaintop views, and be in that environment with the people I love most. But how do you set your mind on somewhere you've never been and something you haven't experienced yet?

Martin Luther put it bluntly: "We know no more about eternal life than children in the womb of their mother know about the world they are about to enter."[9] Of course, the Bible does tell us many things about what heaven will be like, as we consider in the chapters to follow. But on the level of our *experience*, Luther is spot-on.

---

[9] Martin Luther, quoted in Michael Wittmer, "Introduction," in *Four Views on Heaven*, ed. Michael Wittmer (Grand Rapids, MI: Zondervan, 2022), 15.

The only way to long for a *place* you've never been is to long for the *person* whose presence makes that place what it is to you.

Paul sees love for heaven as an extension of our love for Jesus. So long as he is there, we can't possibly be satisfied here. And so long as we aren't fully with him here, we keep our minds set there. Love for Christ anchors us to the future we've been promised, and it reshapes how we live here in the present. Love, in other words, transforms our relationship to space and time.

The writer James Baldwin once captured this transforming power of love with a beautiful thought experiment. Pretend for a moment that you were born in Chicago, that you have never been to Hong Kong, and that until now you've never had remote interest in even visiting that city. Pretend that somehow, unexpectedly, you cross paths with someone who lives in Hong Kong, you fall in love, and your lover returns home without you. What then? "Hong Kong will immediately cease to be a name and become the center of your life." With Paul's words in mind, consider how Baldwin drives his point home:

> You will, I assure you, as long as space and time divide you from anyone you love, discover a great deal about shipping routes, airlines, earth quake, famine, disease, and war. And you will always know what time it is in Hong Kong, for you love someone who lives there. And love will simply have no choice but to go into battle with space and time and, furthermore, to win.[10]

Ultimately, what should drive us to set our minds on heaven is the simple fact that Christ is there and that life apart from him is not

10 James Baldwin, *Nothing Personal* (Boston: Beacon, 1964), 46–47.

enough for us. We can't live without him. One day we won't have to. And until that day, it is our love for him that compels us to gird up our loins and fight the good fight of faith. We go to battle with space and time. I mean for this book to help you fight that battle day by day, for a living and life-shaping hope that nothing can touch.

The Plan of the Book

Before we turn to the chapters ahead, it's worth giving two major clarifications about what to expect.

First, let me be clear about why I'm using the word *heaven* and what I mean by this word when I do. I'm using *heaven* because it's still the most common and most simple term for summing up God's future plans for his people in his world. By *heaven* I don't mean a spiritual place as opposed to the material world we live in now. Rather, I mean the *world to come* as opposed to the *world as it is*. I don't mean a bodiless cloud land our souls fly to when we die. I mean the sum total of all that God has promised us for our ultimate future.

Sometimes that future is described as the new heavens and new earth because it will be so far removed from the brokenness of our world that it may as well be a brand-new beginning.

Other times it's described as a renewal of our world because it will wonderfully expand on everything good and beautiful about this world that God made so well and loves so much.[11]

---

11 I appreciate how theologian Michael Allen sums this up, supported by helpful biblical examples: "The Bible speaks in two diverse ways about redemption, sometimes using concepts like new creation, at other times using imagery of restoration. . . . Salvation ushers in something so radically new that it can be likened to starting from scratch, a completely new creation, as it were. Salvation comes to *this* person or *that* people, however, bringing redeeming grace to them in their unique identities and in ways that involve personal

Most important of all, at the center of the world to come is the promise that God will be there. Heaven is almost synonymous with God himself. That's because all its glory flows from his direct, unmediated presence. The presence of God makes heaven a world of *more*: more happiness and more holiness, fullness of joy forever, an eternal world of love. And the presence of God makes heaven a world of *no more*: no more sin, no more sorrow, no more pain, no more death, and no more tears because God will wipe them away and make sure there is no more reason to weep again. When I use the word *heaven*, I have all this in mind. Heaven is where the presence of God makes all things new.

Second, let me explain what sort of book on heaven this is. The book's subtitle sums up the book's approach: *Meditations on the World to Come for Life in the Meantime*. This is not a systematic breakdown of everything the Bible says about heaven. It is a series of meditations on how the Bible applies the hope of heaven to life in the meantime. I won't tell you everything you may want to know about the world to come; I want to tell you what you need to know to live in hope now.

Each chapter takes up some specific aspect of the Bible's teaching on our future, viewing the same diamond from one angle after another. I hope to make the beauty of these promises more visible and the power of these promises more relatable by connecting them back to the pressures and longings we're living with now.

If you already have a lot of questions about what heaven will be like, I'm afraid you may not find them answered here. I won't take up views on the millennium or on when Jesus will come back. I won't be talking about what the weather will be like on the new

---

continuity, as in a renovation project" ("A Heaven on Earth Perspective," in Wittmer, *Four Views*, 116–17, emphasis original).

earth, or how we will get around, or what sort of clothes we will wear, or whether our pets will be there. It isn't that questions like these are not worth asking. It's that questions like these are beside the point I want to drive home. My goal is to raise the key questions that heaven answers for readers who may not be asking any questions at all. To cultivate your longing for the world to come, it helps to start with what Peter Kreeft calls "the presence of an absence."[12]

With that in mind, most of the chapters follow the same basic arc. I begin by showing what is missing in our lives if this world is everything and there's nothing more to hope for. Then, I insert the hope of heaven into that void, like a key into a lock. Finally, I bring the hope of heaven back into our experience of life in the meantime. The point, chapter by chapter, is to show the difference the perspective of heaven can make to how we view and experience everything else.

---

12 Peter Kreeft, *Heaven: The Heart's Deepest Longing* (New York: Harper & Row, 1980), 29.

1

Bound for Fullness of Joy

How the Hope of Heaven Reframes Our
Dissatisfaction in the Meantime

NEAR THE END OF THE LAST CENTURY, Mississippi physician-turned-novelist Walker Percy reflected on the unique challenge facing writers like himself, compared to earlier novelists like Charles Dickens or John Steinbeck. When Steinbeck wrote about the Okies who lost everything in the Depression and then traveled west for better lives in California, he could bank on clear understanding of what had gone wrong and what could be done about it. His readers could see where poverty comes from and what poverty feels like. They could grasp how better land and more jobs promised a better future for anyone able to survive the journey.

But novelists like Percy had to write about the Okies' great-grandkids. On the terms of Steinbeck's story, these folks have won. They have everything Steinbeck's characters set out to gain and "everything they seem to want," but they seem "ready any minute to slide physically and spiritually into the Pacific Ocean." The novelist today, trying to make sense of middle-class American life, is like a psychiatrist "gazing at a patient who in one sense lives in the best of all possible worlds and yet is suffering from a depression and anxiety which he doesn't understand."[1] The challenge, as Percy put it elsewhere, was to bring to the page what he called a "death in life, of people who seem to be living lives which are good by all sociological standards and yet who somehow seem more dead than alive."[2]

Percy wrote that in 1977. What he noticed then is no less obvious today and no less confusing. The signs are all over the place. We are not as satisfied as we think we ought to be.

About ten years ago, I came across an insightful book called *The Progress Paradox*, by social commentator Gregg Easterbrook. He looks at statistics on a whole host of quality-of-life issues such as health care, disposable income, housing, food security, and affordable leisure activities. On one measure after another, life has gotten better and better—not for everyone but for a huge swath of people all over the world. At the same time, on the same arc, we are reporting greater levels of depression and anxiety than ever before, a restlessness and *unease* with life that is most pronounced among young people, with no end in sight.[3]

As rising prosperity has spread to more and more people around the world, it hasn't led to more and more satisfaction with life.

---

1 Walker Percy, "The State of the Novel: Dying Art or New Science?," in *Signposts in a Strange Land*, ed. Patrick H. Samway (New York: Farrar, Straus, and Giroux, 1991), 141.

2 Walker Percy, "Novel-Writing in an Apocalyptic Time," in *Signposts*, 162.

3 Gregg Easterbrook, *The Progress Paradox: How Life Gets Better While People Feel Worse* (New York: Random House, 2004). Jean Twenge argues that Gen Z adults tend toward a hopeless view of the future and the sense that things are worse now than ever before, despite marked social advantages compared to Gen X or boomers at their stage of life, much less young adults in previous centuries. See Twenge, *Generations: The Real Differences between Gen Z, Millennials, Gen X, Boomers, and Silents—and What They Mean for America's Future* (New York: Atria, 2023), 418–24.

It has led to more and more people learning the same lesson the privileged author of Ecclesiastes learned several thousand years ago. The more resources you have at your disposal, the more opportunities you have to learn that what you think you want isn't really what you want. "All is vanity and a striving after wind" (Eccl. 1:14).

Has there ever been a time when you didn't feel like you were missing something? Have you ever reached the goal you were working toward, grabbed hold of what you were stretching for, and thought to yourself, "That's it. I'm good now"? I haven't.

What do you think it would take to feel truly satisfied?

Augustine boiled down happiness to having and holding what you love—to fully possess the thing you desire and to keep it, without the threat of loss.[4] That sounds right to me. And that's precisely what we're never allowed in this world as it is.

There's always something missing in what we have. And what we have is never ours to keep. In this life our greatest joys are only ever partial and temporary. I had an amazing time in my many years as a full-time student. I also remember what it was like to have those years clouded by the desire for a paying job, a family, and a host of other wonderful possibilities that still lay shrouded in the future. I have a lot of those good gifts now, and I experience deep joy in having them. But that joy is affected by the weight of responsibilities they come with. For now, the fun of having small kids at home is colored by the exhaustion of taking care of them. But when my kids are grown up and eventually fly the nest, I know I'll long to have them back in diapers.

---

4 You'll find these themes scattered throughout Augustine's *Confessions*, but I owe this consolidation to Martin Hägglund, citing Augustine's *Eighty-Three Different Questions*, in *This Life: Secular Faith and Spiritual Freedom* (New York: Anchor, 2019), 71.

That is life in this world as it is, even in the best of times—perhaps especially in the best of times. C. S. Lewis captures this as well as anyone I have read:

> Most people, if they had really learned to look into their own hearts, would know that they do want, and want acutely, something that cannot be had in this world. There are all sorts of things in this world that offer to give it to you, but they never quite keep their promise. The longings which arise in us when we first fall in love, or first think of some foreign country, or first take up some subject that excites us, are longings which no marriage, no travel, no learning, can really satisfy. I am not now speaking of what would be ordinarily called unsuccessful marriages, or holidays, or learned careers. I am speaking of the best possible ones. There was something we grasped at, in that first moment of longing, which just fades away in the reality. I think everyone knows what I mean. The wife may be a good wife, and the hotels and scenery may have been excellent, and chemistry may be a very interesting job: but something has evaded us.[5]

Surely you can relate to what Lewis is describing. How do we account for the fact that we all have longings nothing in this world can satisfy? How did we get here? And what can we do about it?

In this chapter, I want to show you how the Bible accounts for this basic human experience—why we're so dissatisfied now, why full satisfaction is guaranteed in heaven, and how the hope of

---

5   C. S. Lewis, *Mere Christianity* (1952; repr., New York: HarperCollins, 2001), 136.

heaven reframes dissatisfaction in the meantime. To do that, I want to draw from Psalm 16, one of the Bible's earliest expressions of hope for endless joy in the presence of God. But first we need to understand the painful reality that lies behind the psalm.

Why We're So Dissatisfied

The overarching story of the Bible explains how we got here, and that story is in the backdrop of David's prayer in Psalm 16:2:

You are my Lord;
   I have no good apart from you.

No good apart from you. David speaks as one who has learned the hard way a truth we were made to know by instinct. Behind these words lies the garden of Eden and the crucial truth about how God designed us and how sin has distorted us.

In Genesis 1–2, God created the heavens and the earth. Nothing exists apart from God's decision to make something outside himself. And everything that exists reflects the goodness of the one who made it. Genesis walks us through God's creation step by step. God looked at what he made and called it good. The sky is good. The sun, moon, and stars are all good. The land and the sea are good. So is everything in them, from the smallest insect to the largest whale.

But when God made man and woman, Adam and Eve, he called them *very good*. He made them in his image to have a special role in his world and to enjoy a special relationship with him. He fed them delicious food from all around them. In giving them one another, he gave them friendship, marriage, sex, and eventually children. He gave them meaningful work to do. And at the center of all this goodness, he gave them himself. His presence was there with them, in the garden, day by day.

All this points to a crucial aspect of God's original design for humanity in his world. Only humans were made not just to reflect God's goodness but to recognize his goodness through experience and, even more, to relate to him through it. Humans alone were made to "taste and see that *the LORD* is good" (Ps. 34:8). Every creature in the world exists to glorify God, whose genius and power made all things. It is the chief end of humanity to glorify God and *enjoy* him forever.

In the garden, Adam and Eve did exactly what they were made to do. They enjoyed all these good gifts with full knowledge of where all this goodness came from, whose world they were living in, and who they were to him. In the garden, because of God's presence, there was no confusion between the giver and his good gifts. There was no good apart from God, and they knew it.

Until they didn't. The fall of Adam and Eve into sin in Genesis 3 broke this perfect relationship. The serpent tempted Eve with fruit that God had forbidden. This fruit looked good in her eyes, and the serpent told her she ought to have it. His lie introduced a new possibility never before considered: God is a threat to what is good rather than the source. When Adam and Eve took what God had not given for the very first time, they grasped at good apart from God and unleashed hell on earth. Their disobedience brought separation between God and humanity and, along with that, distorted our relationship to God's good gifts.

The reason we are so relentlessly dissatisfied is that sin separates us from the presence of God, and apart from his presence, our relationship to his good world is distorted too. Psalm 16:4 uses language taken straight from the curse in Genesis 3: "The sorrows of those who run after another god shall multiply." Grasp at good apart from God and every good thing comes laced with sorrow. Childbirth is painful. Work is frustrating and often futile. Life itself is now shadowed by death. And through it all, we're still surrounded by good, but apart from God, nothing good is good enough.

Not long ago I had the chance to speak at a conference hosted on the Mediterranean island of Rhodes, just off the coast of Turkey. In between sessions, exploring around the island, I took in some of the most beautiful things my eyes have ever seen. I walked among ancient Greek ruins. I toured the medieval city and its massive castle where the Knights of St. John once kept their headquarters. I ate exquisite local food. And everywhere I went, I saw the jagged coastline up against the stunning beauty of the sea and shades of blue no camera could capture. It was an incredible experience. But the whole time I was there, because my family wasn't with me, I couldn't shake the sense that it was all somehow less real. It was as if only part of me was seeing all that I was seeing. I wanted to look at that sea and share those meals with my wife. I knew how thrilled my boys would have been wandering those cobblestone streets, climbing the city walls, and playing knights up and down the halls of that castle. Without them, I was surrounded by so much goodness yet somehow separated from it. I couldn't be satisfied apart from them.

That's something like what it means for us to live in this world now, without the presence of God among us. We can't deny the goodness we experience, but we long for something more, something that always evades us, as Lewis put it. But there is good news baked into these longings. Our relentless dissatisfaction is a lingering sign of our capacity to be truly satisfied. The memory of the garden is etched on our souls. We feel like this world should be so much more because it should be. It used to be. And one day, through Jesus, it will be again.

Why Heaven Will Be So Satisfying

At the center of the Bible's teaching on the world to come is the promise that God himself will be there. In that world, the separation that sin caused—between ourselves and God, between ourselves and our world, between the giver and all his wonderful gifts—will be erased forever.

Everything good about heaven flows from the presence of God.[6] In a way, every chapter in this book explores from one angle after another why it is so good to be with God, seeing and enjoying him face-to-face. The hope of God's presence is a theme that runs throughout the Bible.

In Psalm 42, for example, the psalmist compares himself to a deer panting after water:

My soul thirsts for God,
for the living God.
When shall I come and appear before God? (42:2)

---

6 Millard Erickson is especially crisp on this point: "Heaven is, first and foremost, the presence of God." *Christian Theology*, unabridged, one-vol. ed. (Grand Rapids, MI: Baker, 1985), 1228; cf. 1226–34. Wayne Grudem agrees: "Heaven is the place where God most fully makes known his presence to bless." Later he continues: "More important than all the physical beauty of the heavenly city, more important than the fellowship we will enjoy eternally with all God's people from all nations and all periods in history, more important than our freedom from pain and sorrow and physical suffering, and more important than reigning over God's kingdom—more important by far than any of these will be the fact that we will be in the presence of God and enjoying unhindered fellowship with him." *Systematic Theology: An Introduction to Biblical Doctrine* (Grand Rapids, MI: Zondervan, 1994), 1159, 1163. The centrality of God's presence is also a theme across the different perspectives on heaven in *Four Views on Heaven*, ed. Michael Wittmer (Grand Rapids, MI: Zondervan, 2022).

Or consider David's prayer in Psalm 63:

O God, you are my God; earnestly I seek you;
  my soul thirsts for you;
my flesh faints for you,
  as in a dry and weary land where there is no water. (63:1)

The prophets promise that one day, beyond the disaster of exile, God will once again live among his people: "My dwelling place shall be with them, and I will be their God, and they shall be my people" (Ezek. 37:27).

Jesus was born as Immanuel, God with us, the Word made flesh to dwell among us and show us his glory. He described himself as the only way back to God, who went to the cross to prepare a place for his friends so that they could be with him where he is (John 14:1–6).

And the Bible ends with a description of a city to match the garden it began with, a whole new world pictured as a holy, new Jerusalem coming down to earth, a city joyous, safe, and unspeakably beautiful because the presence of God spreads all through it:

Then I saw a new heaven and a new earth, for the first heaven and the first earth had passed away, and the sea was no more. And I saw the holy city, new Jerusalem, coming down out of heaven from God, prepared as a bride adorned for her husband. And I heard a loud voice from the throne saying, "Behold, the dwelling place of God is with man. He will dwell with them, and they will be his people, and God himself will be with them as their God. He will wipe away every tear from their eyes, and death shall be no more, neither shall there be mourning, nor crying, nor pain anymore, for the former things have passed away." (Rev. 21:1–4)

But if it's crystal clear that the presence of God is at the center of a biblical hope for heaven, it's still worth asking what makes this presence such good news? What is it about being with God that fires this longing that we see throughout the Bible?

One of the first passages in the Bible to hold out this hope is Psalm 16. And in this psalm, David builds to a conclusion that applies the hope of God's presence to the ache for satisfaction that we've been talking about in this chapter.

> Therefore my heart is glad, and my whole being rejoices;
> my flesh also dwells secure.
> For you will not abandon my soul to Sheol,
> or let your holy one see corruption.
>
> You make known to me the path of life;
> in your presence there is fullness of joy;
> at your right hand are pleasures forevermore. (Ps. 16:9–11)

David expresses his hope that God won't let death have the last word: "You will not abandon my soul to Sheol" (16:10). Sheol is Hebrew shorthand for the grave and the ultimate separation it threatens from our bodies, from this world, and from God himself. David knows God won't let the separation stand. He will bridge the gap that sin has opened.

Then David celebrates what God will do instead: "You make known to me the path of life" (16:11). Where does this path lead? What sort of life are we talking about? "In your presence there is fullness of joy; at your right hand are pleasures forevermore." En-joying God's gifts in God's presence equals *fullness* of joy that lasts *forever*. Remember how Augustine summed up what it would take to be happy? To fully *have* and forever *hold* what we love. In the world to come, through the presence of God, that is precisely the joy we will know. God's presence makes heaven a world of pure and perfect satisfaction.

I can't possibly imagine what it will mean to see God face-to-face. But the psalmist says in God's presence we'll know *fullness* of joy, while here we're always left wanting more. That I can understand. I know the difference between hearing Beethoven's Fifth Symphony as a ringtone and hearing it performed by a world-class orchestra in a perfectly designed symphony hall. I know the difference between watching a movie on an airplane with free headphones and watch-ing a movie in an IMAX theater. I know the difference between getting a text from a friend and a phone call, or the difference between a phone call and a video call, or the difference between a video call and an hour with my friend over coffee. The contexts are different, the clarity of communication is different, and if I love that person, the joy is different. All these formats connect me to my friend, but a lot more of him comes through in person over coffee.

All the good things that don't satisfy us here and now are like a text message version of God's goodness. He is coming through to us in part, and of course all communication is a worthy gift we don't deserve. But we are right to crave more. Then and there, we'll have it. We will worship him by enjoying him in and through the new world he will create to help us know him more. Old Testa-ment scholar Derek Kidner sums up the promise of Psalm 16 like this: "The joys and pleasures are presented as wholly satisfying and endlessly varied, for they are found in both *what he is* and *what he gives*—joys of his . . . presence and of his right hand."[7] To be in God's presence is to enjoy God through all his good gifts without the alienation or the threat of loss that haunts our best days here on earth.

To long for heaven, then, is to long for a place in which everything we love about this world is wonderfully expanded and perfectly fulfilled. And at this point it's worth bringing up one common confusion people have about what heaven will be like. Some Scripture passages about the world to come describe us as eating and drinking, as talking to friends and doing good work, as playing music and taking in beautiful scenery, and other things that we enjoy so much about life in this world now.[8] Then there are passages that talk about worshiping God, praising him, singing songs like we do in church.[9] It's only natural to wonder, which is it? Will we spend eternity worshiping God? Or will we spend eternity doing more of the things we enjoy so much about life now?

It's an understandable confusion that often stems from an understandable concern. As is, we tend to think of worship as a time when we press pause on many of the things we love most about life. We may tack on a potluck, but apart from Communion we don't eat or drink during a worship gathering. We don't talk to friends. We don't get to take in the beauty of creation besides what we can glimpse through a few windows (if we have them). I could go on, but surely you can relate. If heaven is a world of unending worship, it's all too easy to imagine it as a diminishment of our world—not a wonderful renewal and expansion of it.

---

7   Derek Kidner, *Psalms 1–72*, Kidner Classic Commentaries (Downers Grove, IL: InterVarsity Press, 2008), 103.
8   See, for example, Isa. 25:6–9; 65:17–25; Matt. 25:23; 1 Thess. 4:14–18; Rev. 21:9–21.
9   See, for example, the scenes of worship throughout Revelation (5:9–14; 15:1–4).

Will we spend our time contemplating God in all his wondrous attributes, or will we also put our hands to meaningful work? Do we have to sit still in a pew for all eternity? Or can we carry on having fun?

The short answer is I don't know what we'll be seeing or singing, what we'll be doing with all our time, or what it will feel like being there. But some of our confusion and worry comes from the assumption that we can be enjoying good things in the world *or* worshiping God but not both.

In heaven, in a way perfect beyond all imagining, we won't have to choose. We will be finished, once and for all, with any competition between love for the giver and love for his gifts. There will be no possibility of confusion between creatures and the Creator who's glorified in them.

In God's presence, everything we love most about his gifts in this world will be wonderfully, unimaginably expanded. And in God's presence, every fear of loss will be completely, absolutely eliminated. Only in God's presence can we be satisfied because only there will we fully have and forever hold what we love.

Living in the Meantime

Perhaps what strikes me most about David's prayer in Psalm 16 is this: even though he's looking ahead to a forever fullness still to come, he's glad and rejoicing already. "Therefore my heart *is* glad, and my whole being *rejoices*" (16:9). David is drawing true joy now from the fullness of joy he expects to experience later. And the key to that joy is that he has learned to recognize the presence of God in his life now, as a foretaste of his unmediated presence then. The thread that ties present and partial joys to future and permanent joy is the God whose goodness comes through in every good thing. "The LORD is my chosen portion and my cup," David says in 16:5. "I have set the LORD always before me; because he is at my right hand, I shall not be shaken" (16:8). He can see and savor the Lord in his life *now*. He has learned to long for him, to recognize him, and to truly enjoy him now wherever he can, as he waits to enjoy him fully and forever. The "path of life" (16:11) has opened to him already and, as Kidner says, "leads without a break into God's presence and into eternity."[10]

In this final section, I want to think through how we can share David's joy in the present while we wait for what's still to come. To that end, it helps to think of satisfaction as a spectrum—not as something you have or don't have but something you experience more or less in any given season or situation. How can the promise of full satisfaction through the presence of God in heaven deepen the satisfaction you experience in the meantime? It does so by teaching us to accept three crucial truths about life in this world for now.

We Can't Be Fully Satisfied for Now

On this side of heaven, apart from God's presence, we can't be fully satisfied. It's simply not possible. Fullness of joy has to wait. But we will experience more or less satisfaction in the meantime to whatever extent we accept that fact or fight against it. When we grasp at fullness forever in every good thing we see, our satisfaction in life only ever goes down.

Living in a modern, capitalist society, it is absolutely crucial for us to know that our dissatisfaction problem is not one of *possession*— I'm not happy because I haven't yet bought *that*. The problem is one

---

10 Kidner, *Psalms 1–72*, 103.

of *proximity*—I'm not satisfied because I'm not yet in the presence of God. Only there will I know fullness of joy.

When we're not clear about the root cause of our dissatisfaction, we will be carried along by the irresistible wave of consumption into one attempt after another to buy our way into happiness. It's not just that this won't solve the problem we're feeling in our hearts. It's that this will only make the problem worse. When we grasp our way toward happiness, we will only prove again and again that there is nothing for the ache here on earth.

I appreciate how sociologist Hartmut Rosa warns of the distinctly modern instincts about happiness that are ruining our ability to enjoy even the best things about life under the sun. He talks about the unshakable human desire for what he calls "resonance"— a closer relationship with and deeper experience of something beyond ourselves. We sense our separation from something *more*, and we long to close the gap. The problem, he says, is that capitalism translates "our existential need for resonance, our desire for relationships, into a desire for objects."[11] Our mistake is confusing possession with proximity. We think we can buy the satisfaction we're longing for, locking it down on our terms.

There are good reasons why there are so many outlet malls near the beach and why every national park features a thriving gift shop. People go to Yellowstone for resonance—to stand in awe and feel their own smallness compared to the untold age and vast scale of all this beauty. But wouldn't it be nice to take some of that home in a T-shirt or a water bottle sticker?

The problem, Rosa argues, is that we're grasping at vapor. The more we buy, the more we want, and the more we buy again. The

---

11 Hartmut Rosa, *The Uncontrollability of the World* (Cambridge, UK: Polity, 2020), 38.

only thing that grows through all our grasping is not our share of the world or our enjoyment of it but the markets that thrive on this lust for heaven on earth.

So much better, then, to accept that we can't hoard our way into fullness of joy. God must give it to us, when he gives us the gift of his presence. When we do, another possibility opens up for us in the meantime, which brings me to the second truth we must accept.

God's Gifts Don't Last for Now

Have you noticed, since the rise of the smartphone camera, the difference between soaking up a wonderful moment and trying to capture it with the perfect shot? Maybe it's a mountaintop view, a family gathering, or a sporting event. It's so easy now to look at whatever we're seeing through the few square inches of glass and liquid crystal that we're holding in front of our faces. We want so badly to capture the moment—to make it ours and to make it last. But what do we actually end up with? An image so terribly shrunk down that it's barely worth looking at, and most of us don't. Meanwhile, even in the moment, our joy in the experience is shrunk down too, clouded by the quest for the perfect shot and hemmed in by the size of the screen we're using to frame it. We enjoy the moment more when we just accept that it won't last, that we can't possibly fully capture it, and that we may as well soak it up while we can. There's a powerful metaphor here for life overall.

You can find ancient wisdom from all over the world telling you to prioritize the present over the past or the future. And these days mindfulness is a multibillion-dollar industry. Who doesn't want to work on living in the moment?

But how do you actually do it? How do you truly savor what's right in front of you and keep it from being overwhelmed by grief over what you no longer have or longing for what you don't have yet? You need to know that the best thing about every good thing on earth is the God whose goodness shines through it. There is no good apart from him. And there is no end to the goodness he intends to share of himself with his people.

The impulse to capture and hoard what we love flattens the world like a smartphone camera flattens an ocean backdrop. That impulse is rooted in false assumptions about reality. It assumes that this world is ultimate and its goodness a nonrenewable resource in short supply. It reflects a scarcity mindset. You stock up water in the Arizona desert. You don't do that in the Mississippi Delta.

With the perspective of heaven, we can see things more clearly. There is no scarcity of goodness in God. When good gifts on earth are seen as they are in themselves, apart from God, they will be defined by all they are not. They don't fully satisfy. They don't last forever. They can't be all we want them to be. But what if we see *God's* goodness in them? Then we know whatever good things we taste now, however fleeting, come from an overflowing, never-ending stream that keeps on giving.

God himself is the gift within all gifts. He means to satisfy us completely in his presence, in his time. Knowing this truth makes all the difference in our experience of partial and temporary pleasures here and now. We don't have to always be looking over our shoulders, asking ourselves, "Is that all?" Now we can be always looking ahead and thinking, "I can't wait to see what's next." Look for God's goodness in whatever he gives you. Taste the pleasures of his right hand now, wherever you can, while you wait for the fullness of joy that lasts forever in his presence. All this leads to one more truth for life in the meantime.

Dissatisfaction Is a Friend for Now

Living now in the hope of heaven with the promise of fullness of joy in God's own presence means leaning into dissatisfaction while we wait. Sometimes when my wife and I go out to dinner and a movie, we are suckered in by the popcorn. If we start with the movie, we pull into the theater looking forward to dinner. Maybe we even have a spot picked out in advance. Then we open the door to the theater, and the smell quite simply overwhelms us. The taste of the popcorn never lives up to the promise of that smell, but we're suckers for it over and over, especially when we're hungry already. More times than I can tell, we've ruined our appetites by gorging on bottomless popcorn that couldn't possibly compare to the meal we were looking forward to. When we treat our hunger like an enemy to be neutralized as soon as possible, we miss out on what would have been so much better. When we leave our hunger where it is, even cultivate it over the course of a movie, we're more ready than ever for the joy of that meal when it comes.

What makes the modern world go round is our temptation to throw everything we can muster at dissatisfaction, chasing the wind as if there's something out there somewhere that can take the edge off our hunger. There isn't. And God means for this to help us. Our hunger for something more is a precious ally, drawing us on toward the feast that is sure to come.

In *The Problem of Pain*, C. S. Lewis writes beautifully of how God uses dissatisfaction to protect us from nesting here and to preserve us for the true home he has prepared:

> The settled happiness and security which we all desire, God
> withholds from us by the very nature of the world: but joy,

pleasure, and merriment He has scattered broadcast. . . . The security we crave would teach us to rest our hearts in this world and oppose an obstacle to our return to God: a few moments of happy love, a landscape, a symphony, a merry meeting with friends, a bathe or a football match, have no such tendency. Our Father refreshes us on the journey with some pleasant inns, but will not encourage us to mistake them for home.[12]

The temporary joys scattered throughout our lives are precious gifts to refresh us on our journey. But God loves us too much to let us mistake them for home. For now, settled rest means mortal danger. He wants us restless, sober, watching, and waiting.

This side of heaven, with the perspective of heaven, our dissatisfaction is a gift we would be foolish to squander. In a way it is, as philosopher Peter Kreeft puts it, "the greatest thing on earth because it leads us to heaven, which is the greatest thing of all."[13]

---

12 C. S. Lewis, *The Problem of Pain* (New York: Collier, 1962), 115.
13 Peter Kreeft, *Heaven: The Heart's Deepest Longing* (New York: Harper & Row, 1980), 37.

2

Bound for Spotless Righteousness

How the Hope of Heaven Overcomes Our
Feelings of Inadequacy in the Meantime

I DON'T KNOW WHERE IT CAME FROM, but now it seems to
be everywhere. I hear it on podcasts and TV shows. I've seen it
on T-shirts and social media graphics. A quick search for it on
Amazon brings up hundreds of results, ranging from books for
kids and adults to silver charm bracelets to hoodies of many colors
to embroidered makeup cases to wall hangings and throw pillows
and stickers to place on your rearview mirror. I'm talking about
the simple, uplifting mantra for our times: "You Are Enough."

Surely you've seen this too. But have you stopped to consider
why this phrase, in these settings, is this popular? I see at least two
implications.

For one thing, it means that insecurity about our worth is a massive problem in our culture. I'm not just talking about how wide
the problem must reach if this phrase is popping up all over the
place. I'm talking about how deep the problem must go. Just how

low must my self-view be if I get a boost from a statement made by who knows who, about no one in particular, and mass-produced for sale at suburban homegoods megastores?

The popularity of this phrase fits perfectly with what French sociologist Alain Ehrenberg argues in *The Weariness of the Self*, his history of depression among contemporary Western people. It's not a book about how to cope with depression, all the mysterious factors that cause it, or how to get rid of it. It's a book about what depressed people are saying about themselves, about how they are describing their experience.

He believes depression has spread the way it has, when and where it has, because of the cultural expectation that it's up to each individual to define the meaning and value of his own life. The defining feature of modern depression, based on interviews of those who are suffering, is a suffocating sense of inadequacy. Here's how Ehrenberg puts it: "Depression presents itself as an illness of responsibility in which the dominant feeling is that of failure. The depressed individual is unable to measure up; he is tired of having to become himself. . . . The depressed person is a person out of gas."[1]

Whatever else you may say about it, "You Are Enough" is a symptom of a deep and pervasive problem in our culture. Many people feel relentlessly, hopelessly inadequate and long for relief.

The second thing this phrase suggests is that we humans have an inevitable craving for validation. We desperately want to measure up. We need to hear from someone else that we do. And it's entirely appropriate that we should. The theological category for the validation we crave is *justification*. Think of it like a courtroom where a judge gives a verdict on your standing before him. The

---

1 Alain Ehrenberg, *The Weariness of the Self: Diagnosing the History of Depression in the Contemporary Age* (Montreal: McGill-Queen's University Press, 2010), 4.

biblical vocabulary word for a statement like "You Are Enough" is *righteous*. To be righteous is to have right standing before the proper authority, to have a life that measures up. It is being exactly what you're supposed to be. When you are righteous, you are enough.

We are not wrong to crave justification. It is supposed to matter to us whether we're good enough. This is core to our humanity. But everything depends on where we look for this validation, on what basis, and when.

The only person authorized to tell us that we are enough is the God who gave us our lives in the first place. Right at the heart of the gospel is the promise that God already sees us as righteous because of Jesus's righteousness received through faith. Paul says in Romans that "since we *have been* justified by faith, we *have* peace with God through our Lord Jesus Christ" (5:1). That means there is "*now* no condemnation for those who are in Christ Jesus" (8:1). Justification is something we already have if we're in Christ, a guarantee of our righteous standing before God that we must remember and rest in every day.

And yet the gospel also looks forward. "By faith," Paul writes, "we ourselves *eagerly wait* for the hope of righteousness" (Gal. 5:5). Like so much of what God has promised us, justification has an *already* and a *not-yet* dimension. *Already* by faith we are righteous in God's sight because of Jesus. But we are waiting for righteousness too. We do *not yet* see ourselves as God sees us. For now, we walk by faith and not by sight. We see our failures with painful clarity, not the spotless righteousness in which Jesus wraps us. On the day of judgment, we will trade our faith for sight once and for all. We will stand before God and receive publicly, unmistakably, and irrevocably what he has promised us already—his pronouncement of our righteousness in Christ. We will know from experience that we are enough not because of what we've done with our lives but because of what Jesus has done with his. On that day, and only on that day, will we be finished wondering whether or not we measure up.[2]

In this chapter I want to help you connect that day to an age-old struggle that is dialed way up in our culture today. I want to connect the hope of judgment day to the everyday struggle with feelings of inadequacy. To do that, we must begin with some account of how this exhausting search for justification has become so exhausting.

The Exhausting Search for Justification

One of the most convincing explanations I've seen for how we got here comes from philosopher Charles Taylor in *The Ethics of Authenticity*. Taylor traces our angst about justification back to massive changes from ancient cultures to our modern world.

In premodern times honor was tied to status, and status was set by birth. Everyone assumed that we're not all equal, and no one did much moving up or down the social ladder. You were born noble with an honor or awesomeness everyone recognized, or you were not. Either way, you were who you were.

---

2 I appreciate the way Thomas Schreiner summarizes the past and future dimensions to justification in the Bible. He lists many texts that speak of justification as a future reality, tied to the final judgment (Rom. 2:13; 8:33; 1 Cor. 4:4–5; Gal. 2:16–17; 5:5; Phil. 3:9). And he lists many texts that refer to justification as a past reality, claimed by faith (Rom. 5:1, 9, 17; 8:30; 1 Cor. 1:30; 6:11; 2 Cor. 5:21; Titus 3:7). Then he sums up the biblical teaching on the timing of justification: "Believers in Jesus Christ are now justified through faith in Jesus Christ. They are justified by faith alone by virtue of Christ's death for their sins and his resurrection for their justification (Rom. 4:25). Still, they look forward to the day when the declaration will be announced *publicly* and to the entire world. In this sense, as many scholars attest, justification is an already but not yet reality." *Faith Alone: The Doctrine of Justification* (Grand Rapids, MI: Zondervan, 2015), 157. See also 153–57.

For a host of reasons this rigid inequality was not good, and thankfully things are different now. In our modern, egalitarian culture, there is in theory no status assigned at birth. We say that everyone is equal in dignity and free to become whatever they want to become. Anyone can have honor, not just the nobles. But the opportunity to gain status comes with pressure that medieval peasants never had to live with. Now it's up to you, the individual, to craft an identity others may recognize as awesome. In theory, anyone can get the recognition he or she craves, but no one can take it for granted. The modern person has "to win it through exchange, and it can fail."[3]

Taylor is saying that whereas the ancient world had nobles and peasants, our world has winners and losers. Back then your status was set at birth. Now you have to establish your value in a crowded marketplace. And how do you establish value in a crowded marketplace? You're going to need a niche—something the market is looking for that no one else is doing as well as you can do it. You need to find something unique to you, something that matters to others, and you need to do your thing better than anyone else.

Nike founder Phil Knight is a perfect example of the cultural pressure Taylor is talking about. Near the beginning of his memoir, *Shoe Dog*, Knight describes the angst in his twenty-something soul that drove him to pursue what he calls his "Crazy Idea" of founding a shoe company. His father's ultimate goal had always been respectability. "He liked doing a vigorous backstroke each day in the mainstream."[4] Knight wanted above all to stand out from the crowd: "I had an aching sense that our time is short, shorter than

3 Charles Taylor, *The Ethics of Authenticity* (Cambridge, MA: Harvard University Press, 1991), 48.
4 Phil Knight, *Shoe Dog: A Memoir by the Creator of Nike* (New York: Scribner, 2016), 12.

we ever know, short as a morning run, and I wanted mine to be meaningful. And purposeful. And creative. And important. Above all . . . different. I wanted to leave a mark on the world. I wanted to win."[5] Meaningful. Purposeful. Important. This is justification language. He wanted his life to count for something. And the key to that justification is crystal clear: he would have to do something *different*. What makes you different makes you valuable.

There are softer versions of this approach to self-worth, of course. From Disney movies to elementary school mindfulness exercises, kids are told to remind themselves of all the wonderful things about themselves—that they're brave and smart and strong and able to do or be anything they want. But right at the center of what they need to know is that there's no one else exactly like them. They're unique, which is to say special, which is to say worth something. As one educator put it, the goal of self-affirmations is to "make the self firm." It's giving kids the chance to show "the ways in which you are special."[6]

Especially in an elementary school setting, there is much to appreciate in the motives behind affirmations like these. Where schools include hundreds of students from communities dealing with generational poverty, weighed down by centuries of lies told about their dignity and their capacities, these practices aim to set the record straight and to help these precious kids see the truth about themselves. This goal is absolutely crucial.

But however well intentioned, however mixed with truth, this perspective on self-worth relieves one burden by imposing another.

---

5 Knight, *Shoe Dog*, 3.
6 Katie Loos, quoting Stanford professor Geoffrey Cohen, in "How Affirmations Can Support Your Child's Learning," *U.S. News & World Report*, June 30, 2021, https://www .usnews.com/.

It affirms that you have value. But it grounds your value in what makes you unique. Your worth comes from what you are that no one else is. It means to level the field, but instead it feeds relentless competition. All the pressure rests squarely on the shoulders of each individual child.

Ultimately it costs me very little to tell my son that he is the pearl in the oyster of the world. It is as easy as telling someone to order the filet mignon when he's the one picking up the check. I may genuinely care about him, I may sincerely want good for him, but if I say that he's valuable because he's unique, he will have to find where he stands out, and he will have to keep the performance going. He will be the one to pay the bill, not me.

It is no wonder that burnout is such a pervasive problem in our culture. Sociologist Hartmut Rosa traces the problem to this relentless pressure to perform—to figure out what you're good at and to do that thing more and more, better and better. Everyone now has 24-7 access to all the best things other people have going on—their cute kids, their exotic vacations, their new outfits, their enviable book taste, their delicious homemade meals. The pressure to keep up, Rosa says, feels like running up a descending escalator. It wears you out, but you can't stop for breath. If you stop, you're not just resting; you're losing ground every second.[7]

If your worth comes from what you can do, and if the measure is how you compare to others, how could you possibly know when you've done enough? You can't. The search for justification is quite simply, inevitably exhausting.

---

7   We push ourselves to exhaustion and beyond, Rosa argues, because we fear that if we stop, "we lose ground against a highly dynamic environment, with which we are always in competition." Hartmut Rosa, *The Uncontrollability of the World* (Cambridge, UK: Polity, 2020), 10.

The Ultimate Hope for Rest

If you know what it feels like to struggle with inadequacy, then you have experienced longing for the rest you will only fully enjoy in heaven. There we will each stand before the judgment seat of the God who made us, who will give us the validation we have been craving based on what Jesus has done, not what we have done. I want to show you how to leverage this hope for your future into greater freedom in your present.

The apostle Paul lived his life with the day of judgment always on his horizon. He wrote of the coming judgment often throughout his letters. To Timothy he described Jesus as the one "who is to judge the living and the dead" (2 Tim. 4:1). To the Romans he wrote that "we will all stand before the judgment seat of God" (Rom. 14:10). To the Thessalonians he wrote that the "day of the Lord will come like a thief in the night" (1 Thess. 5:2). In his second letter to the Corinthians, he reminded them that "we must all appear before the judgment seat of Christ, so that each one may receive what is due" (2 Cor. 5:10). And in all this, Paul was merely echoing what the rest of the Bible teaches about the end of history and the day the prophets called "the day of the Lord." It is a day on which every person will give an account to God for the lives they have lived, for every thought and deed and attitude, where things now hidden will be revealed before the God who knows all things. It is a day of reckoning based on God's perfect justice. The New Testament speaks of this day too, connecting what the prophets said was coming to the return of Jesus and what he will do when he comes again.

I think it's safe to say, for most Christians most of the time, this day of judgment is not high on the list of things we think about if and when we think about our heavenly future. Everything hidden, now revealed? That is a terrifying thought for anyone with any trace of humble self-awareness. The Bible says there is no one righteous, not even one (Rom. 3:10).

The prophets described the day of the Lord as a day of wrath, a day when God will set right all wrongs that went unpunished in this life, all the things the powerful have done to the weak that no one could stop them from doing. Jesus described this day as a day of weeping and gnashing of teeth, a day when those who have rejected God will receive what they have asked for—lives utterly cut off from the only source of all goodness, truth, beauty, and love.

Yet for Paul, the judgment to come was one he looked to with hope, and this hope made a profound difference to how he looked at himself in the meantime. The best place to see this is Paul's autobiographical before-and-after summary of his life in Philippians 3.

First he looks back at how he saw himself before he came to know Jesus: "If anyone else thinks he has reason for confidence in the flesh, I have more: circumcised on the eighth day, of the people of Israel, of the tribe of Benjamin, a Hebrew of Hebrews; as to the law, a Pharisee; as to zeal, a persecutor of the church; as to righteousness under the law, blameless" (Phil. 3:4–6). This list of qualifications seems well rehearsed to me. There's no chance that this was the first time he thought about how he stacked up against his peers. Paul knew that he was special, and he knew why.

Then everything changed for him when he met Jesus:

Whatever gain I had, I counted as loss for the sake of Christ. Indeed, I count everything as loss because of the surpassing worth of knowing Christ Jesus my Lord. For his sake I have suffered the loss of all things and count them as rubbish, in order that I may gain Christ and be found in him, not having a righteousness of my own that comes from the law, but that which comes through faith in Christ, the righteousness from God that depends on faith—that I may know him and the power of his resurrection, and may share his sufferings, becoming like him in his death, that by any means possible I may attain the resurrection from the dead. (Phil. 3:7–11)

At the center of this passage is Paul's desire to "gain Christ and be found in him." It's a reference to the day of judgment. What gives knowing Christ "surpassing worth"? What makes all that he once took for gain, all those things that once proved his worth, seem worthless by comparison? Paul's confidence that only the righteousness of Jesus will survive the judgment that's coming.

Before Christ, Paul had hoped to stand before God good enough on his own two feet, wrapped in a righteousness all his own, unique to him. Now he wants to stand there good enough in Christ. Now he wants the righteousness that comes from God and depends on faith. And the reason he made this trade is crystal clear. "By any means possible"—by the only means possible—he wants resurrection from the dead.

Paul knows that the wages of sin is death. Death is what he has earned through his own best attempt to be good enough. But eternal life is a free gift of God to all who believe, based on who Jesus is and not who they are. In Jesus, Paul will survive the day of judgment. On his own, he won't.

Whether the day of judgment is good news or bad news comes down to what you will be wearing.[8] Pastor Chris Davis says that the

---

8 The Bible's teaching about the day of judgment also shows that there will be rewards given to believers for their faithfulness in this life, and Paul's warning in 1 Cor. 3 shows that some

righteousness of Jesus is to judgment day what a space suit is to a walk on the moon.[9] The space suit is a standard-issue uniform. You don't get to brag about your fashion sense. Forget about compliments or standing out from the crowd. And nobody cares. This is life and death. You can wear the suit and survive, or you can reject the suit and die.

When God gave his only Son so that those who believe in him would not perish, he sent into the world a righteousness from God that depends on faith. He said, in effect, "Here, wear this and live." Jesus's righteousness is spotless. This Son was such a delight to his Father that on more than one occasion a voice spilled over from heaven, with uncontainable passion, to shout to all the world, "This is my Son! He pleases me!" (see Matt. 3:17; 17:5). All over the Gospels, you can see why. Jesus said it was his food to do his Father's will (John 4:34). He lived on joyful obedience. He prayed to his Father in secret, not to draw attention to himself but because

---

work done by Christians won't survive that day as pleasing to God. This complex topic is beyond the scope of my chapter, but there are a couple of things worth saying here. First, the good works for which we will be rewarded come in response to God's gift of justification by grace; they are not grounds for justification before God or any reason for us to boast in our own worthiness. They testify to our genuine faith, but they do not supplement our standing before God. This is the sequence of Eph. 2:8–10: by grace you are saved through faith, not by works, so that no one can boast. *And* you are created in this grace for good works. Second, if you are in Christ, you have no reason to fear that day. Romans 8:1 is the key: "There is therefore now no condemnation for those who are in Christ Jesus." John Piper describes this promise as "the massive Rock of Gibraltar on which the rewards ceremony will take place." *Come, Lord Jesus: Meditations on the Second Coming of Christ* (Wheaton, IL: Crossway, 2023), 149. Finally, I'm convinced by the argument that the differing rewards in heaven will be differing capacities for joy in all that God is. Everyone in heaven will fully enjoy God. No one will experience lack, much less envy. But some through their sacrifice, through their suffering, through their persecution for Christ, or myriad other acts of faithfulness will be prepared for greater capacity to enjoy the limitless goodness of God. For more on this subject, see Piper's excellent treatment in *Come, Lord Jesus*, 135–59.

9   Chris Davis, *Bright Hope for Tomorrow: How Anticipating Jesus' Return Gives Strength for Today* (Grand Rapids, MI: Zondervan, 2022), 37–38.

he couldn't live without him. He loved him with all his heart, soul, and mind. He treated people with dignity and kindness and compassion even when they had nothing to offer him in return. He was faithful to his friends no matter how many times they let him down. And even those who crucified him had to admit that he did not deserve to die like this. He didn't die because he deserved it. He died willingly because we do.

On the only standard that matters, Jesus's righteousness is spotless. When you're found in him by faith, you are spotless too. Paul believed this to his core. And because he lived his life confidently waiting for the day of judgment, he was not easily bothered by how he measured up to any other standard. His inadequacy was entirely beside the point. Once he wrote to friends in Corinth who had come to believe that he wasn't good enough compared to other teachers who had come into the church behind him. But knowing they saw him as inadequate didn't make him feel inadequate at all. "But with me it is a very small thing that I should be judged by you or by any human court. In fact, I do not even judge myself" (1 Cor. 4:3). Why doesn't he connect how they see him to how he sees himself? Because they are not the standard and this is not the time: "It is the Lord who judges me. Therefore do not pronounce judgment *before the time*, before the Lord comes, who will bring to light the things now hidden in darkness and will disclose the purposes of the heart" (4:4–5). Paul lived his life free from our exhausting search for justification but not because justification didn't matter to him. He was free because he looked for it from the right source at the right time.

What does all this have to do with longing for heaven? When we place our faith in Christ, God sees us as he sees Jesus. Once and for all. "There is therefore now no condemnation for those who are in Christ Jesus. . . . It is God who justifies. Who is to condemn?" (Rom. 8:1, 33–34). But for now, in this world as it is, we don't see ourselves as God sees us. It's so obvious to me that I'm not as patient with my kids as Jesus was with his disciples. I'm not as bothered as he was by the reality of sin overall and much more bothered than he was when someone sins against me. I'm not as kind or compassionate, not as resilient in temptation, not as eager to pray. For as long as I live in this world, when I look at myself I will see plenty of evidence that I am not enough as I am. Paul knew this too. He once called himself the chief of sinners (1 Tim. 1:15). We claim the righteousness of Christ by faith, but we don't enjoy it by sight. Not yet.

But on that day, when Jesus returns to judge the living and the dead, we will stand in him complete. And we will finally and forever see ourselves as the Father sees his only begotten Son. We will receive the commendation Jesus deserves. That is why Paul longs for the day of judgment and why we should too.

The Challenge of Faith in the Meantime

Until Christ comes again, we will face an everyday battle to walk by faith and not by sight. We will live with daily, even hourly, evidence that we aren't good enough on our own. Some of that will come from standards in our culture. Some we've set for ourselves. Some matter to us more than they should. Some will come from our growth in spiritual maturity, as we become more and more sensitive to the seriousness of our sin against God and our neighbors. The question is not whether we will struggle with these feelings but how we will respond to them when we do. Will we walk by faith, waiting patiently for the day when we see ourselves as God sees us in Jesus? Or will we grasp for our own righteousness that we can see here and now? How can we walk by faith while we wait to see what God sees?

Recognize the Temptation of Pride

We need to be honest about the impulse to stand out from the crowd. That impulse is pride. As C. S. Lewis puts it, pride is "essentially competitive" and "gets no pleasure out of having something, only out of having more of it than the next man."[10] Pride says to figure out where you shine, then build your life there.

Pride is the poison our culture doles out as medicine. The standard prescription for dealing with inadequacy is to find what you're good at and lean into it. Build up your confidence in where you're exceptional. This poison only feeds the problem it means to solve. It sickens individuals. It corrupts societies. And it ultimately leads to death.

Recognize the Temptation of Works Righteousness

This poison is in the air we breathe. It lives in our hearts too. We will always be susceptible to pride and looking for a righteousness that is ours, that we can see, based on works.

We are at our most susceptible when we feel inadequate. Just think for a moment how you would normally look to encourage those feeling down on themselves, especially if they are not completely wrong about what's bothering them. Our natural tendency is to want them to overcome what they are feeling bad about by pointing out what they are really good at. We will say things like, "Maybe you're not as fast as that guy, but you're so much stronger." "Maybe you struggle in social studies, but you're amazing at math."

10 C. S. Lewis, *Mere Christianity* (1952; repr., New York: HarperCollins, 2001), 122.

"So you're not the most organized, but you're so creative and intelligent." We want to help them feel better, and our default strategy is probably to help them see what makes them uniquely awesome.

There is even a popular Christian version of this impulse with just enough truth to be dangerous. The idea is that the key to feeling good about yourself is recognizing the unique gifts, strengths, and beauty that God put into you when he made you *you*. "You are as unique as a fingerprint. Your Creator knows exactly how because he's the one who made you this way. You need to see what God sees when he looks at you."

Can you hear in words like these the echo of the Pharisee's prayer, looking over his shoulder at the pitiful tax collector standing nearby? "God, I thank you that I am not like other men" (Luke 18:11). Sure, there's a nod to God's role in his awesomeness. This is, on its surface, a prayer of thanksgiving. But in its substance this prayer is self-worship. It celebrates what makes me *me*, and it feeds on the comparison to others that stirs feelings of inadequacy in the first place. Remember, it was not the Pharisee who went home justified that day. It was the tax collector who faced up to his own inadequacy and simply asked for mercy.

Of course, I don't mean to say there is nothing unique about you and me. I'm not denying that our uniqueness can glorify God by reflecting his wonderful creativity. What I'm saying is that it matters what we want to have noticed and validated.

Because our culture values what our hearts naturally want— my brilliance on display, head and shoulders above the crowd— we will be tempted to see Jesus as something we put on beneath the surface, while we carry on angling for attention to whatever we have to offer the world. We can treat Jesus as a pair of long johns. Warm, comforting, nice to have on a cold winter's day, but not outward facing. We probably can't name the brand and probably don't care whether anyone else shows up wearing the same style. What matters, what's noticeable, is what we put on next. That's where we're more picky.

It's one thing for me to say that all you need is Jesus. It's another thing to say that all I have is Christ. He's not my base layer. He's not my bottom rung on a ladder I hope to climb. He's everything to me—all my righteousness, and therefore, all my hope and peace. All other ground is sinking sand. How can we say that and mean it from the heart?

Remember the Day of Judgment

We need a clear, cultivated, everyday awareness that the day of judgment is coming, and on that day only the righteousness of Jesus will survive. The day of judgment kept Paul humble. He didn't care how he stacked up against Peter or Apollos. It didn't matter to him who the Corinthians would rather have in their pulpit. He refused to live his life as one perpetual trial in their courtroom. He wanted only to be found in Christ, and he would not pass judgment before the time comes.

Think about our desire to stand out from others as a desire for judgment at the wrong time on the wrong basis. We will often want a judgment here and now, and we want it based on what we can see, celebrate, and claim for our own. We would rather live by sight than wait in faith.

But focusing our eyes on the right time—the day of judgment, when we stand before the all-seeing eye and perfect holiness of the only one who matters—helps tether our hearts to the right basis—the spotless righteousness of Jesus, not one of our own making. If something won't matter to God on that day, it shouldn't matter to us now. And all that matters on that day—the only righteousness that measures up—is the righteousness from God that depends on faith.

A few years ago, the *New York Times* ran a story about thousands of articles of clothing found scattered on the ocean floor where they had settled during the sinking of the *Titanic*. When the ship broke apart, "its contents fell more slowly, fluttering to the depths like grim leaf fall. And there, in the lightless saline netherworld, a vest, a trilby hat, a pair of laced boots, a belted valise and an alligator bag (along with a huge range of artifacts) lay scattered across a broad apron of remnants."[11]

The main focus of the article is reflected in its title: "On the Titanic, Defined by What They Wore." These objects reveal so much about the social status of the passengers onboard and how important it was to them to project to everyone else what status they had. "The Titanic was this stage where people were performing certain versions of themselves, for all kinds of audiences."[12]

There is a haunting parable in these discoveries for those with eyes to see. The North Atlantic floor was littered with objects of social status once carefully chosen to make the right statement, to gain the right validation. Every article of clothing, meant in some way to justify those who wore them, could do nothing to protect anyone from the disaster of that night.

After the *Titanic* struck an iceberg and began to sink, the crew passed out life vests to panicked passengers. They weren't much to look at. They were simple and boxy, covered in brown canvas, like wearing a potato sack with armholes and big blocks of cork sewn into the chest. Do you think anyone cared? How many passengers

---

11 Guy Trebay, "On the Titanic, Defined by What They Wore," *New York Times*, April 11, 2012, https://www.nytimes.com/.

12 Trebay, "On the Titanic."

worried that the vests would cover up their tailored tuxedos or designer dresses? Do you think anyone whispered to somebody else, "Can you believe Mable is wearing exactly the same vest as Mary? What a nightmare! How embarrassing!" Of course not. Those fancy suits and dresses wouldn't float. When you know your finest material will only end up on the ocean floor, it doesn't matter how well it measures up to the crowd. You want a life vest, plain and simple. You want to wear what it takes to survive, even if that means you're done standing out.

The day of judgment shows us the storm we are facing, and it drives us to Christ as the only way of escape. Seeing our lives through the lens of that day keeps us desperate to be found in him, though everything else be counted as loss. And knowing that we will be found in him, that one day we'll see ourselves as God sees him, helps us find rest while we wait in the meantime.

3

Bound for Perfect Holiness

How the Hope of Heaven Empowers Our
Battle with Sin in the Meantime

WHEN IT COMES TO handyman projects around the house, at this point in my life I don't even like to try. I'm not proud of this fact about me, but my posture is based on a lot of hard evidence.

All my trying over the years has more than convinced me of some basic facts about pretty much any handyman project that presents itself: This will take longer than I think it will. It will require more materials and cost more money than I expect. The instructional videos will make no sense to me. Because I don't know what I'm doing, I will probably make the problem worse. And in the end, I won't be able to get it done anyway. I'll just be calling whichever one of my handyman friends happens to show up at the wrong time in my text feed.

I know I have basically two choices. I can fail after wasting my time, money, and mental space. Or I can save myself the trouble and accept failure now, on the front end. Why would I fail the hard way when I may as well fail the easy way?

I know how this ends. What I expect from the future has a tremendous effect on my motivation in the present.

I've seen this same dynamic play out time and again in the battle against sin, both in my own heart and in my ministry to others. I don't know of a more powerful barrier to growth in holiness than hopelessness. Especially when the pattern of sin is one you wrestle with for years, it can be so easy to say: I know where this is going. I've tried. I can't stop. It's miserable trying and failing and trying and failing. I want to change but I don't think I can. Why keep fighting only to keep on losing? *I know how this ends.*

If you have ever felt this way, what you've felt is your need for the hope of heaven, where the one who began a good work in you will finish what he started. A couple chapters ago I talked about how right at the center of what the Bible teaches about the world to come is the promise that God will be there—that his people will live in his presence and that every other good thing about heaven flows from that best thing of all. In this chapter I want to show you one specific promise of what the presence of God will mean for those who belong to him. To be in God's presence is to become perfectly holy, just like he is holy. I want to show you why perfect holiness is how this ends for every child of God and how this hope purifies us now in the meantime.

To get there I want to meditate on two verses, 1 John 3:2–3:

> Beloved, we are God's children now, and what we will be has not yet appeared; but we know that when he appears we shall be like him, because we shall see him as he is. And everyone who thus hopes in him purifies himself as he is pure.

I want to draw two simple points from these two simple verses. In heaven, we will be perfected by sight. And on earth, we are being purified by hope.

Perfected by Sight in Heaven

I love the humility in John's setup. We are God's children now. We know that much. We don't know what we'll be like then, when Christ returns and we enter his presence in his new world. But here's one thing we know: "When he appears, we shall be like him, because we shall see him as he is." When we see him as he is, we will be holy as he is holy. Looking at God produces likeness to God. Let's consider this connection one step at a time.

What Will Seeing God Be Like for Us?

First, John says we will see him as he is. This experience is at the heart of what makes heaven heaven, and the longing for this face-to-face vision is scattered throughout the Bible. It's central, that much is clear. But what will it be like? When we see him, what will we be seeing?

The short answer is I don't know. No one does. As John puts it one chapter later, "No one has ever seen God" (1 John 4:12). We do get glimpses in some scenes throughout the Bible. Moses on Mount Sinai. Isaiah in his vision. Peter, James, and John at the transfiguration. Paul on the road to Damascus. What these men saw were glimpses of a reality so powerful that Paul was blinded by it, so glorious that Moses's face shone with its afterglow, and so captivating that Peter wanted to build a house to contain it and keep it going.

On one level, appearances like these simply show us that whatever it will be like to see God, we have never seen anything like it before. That's why John is so humble and straightforward in 1 John 3:2. We don't know what we will be because he hasn't appeared, and we don't know how he will appear.

On another level, though, appearances like these do shed some light on what we should expect. When we see God as he is, we will be seeing something so powerful, so glorious, so captivating that we could not possibly look away. We will be utterly absorbed by his beauty.

Let me pause here and state the obvious. Perhaps because this is all so abstract, this is also where many Christians struggle to feel any sort of longing for heaven. Staring at God all day? Forever? In Isaiah's vision, the angels who serve near God's heavenly throne call out to one another in a loop, "Holy, holy, holy is the Lord of hosts" (Isa. 6:3). Maybe you can enjoy singing that hymn every four to six weeks—but ceaselessly? Maybe, you wonder, is that my future too? Will I *have to*?

If that's what you're thinking so far, let me turn that back around on you: How beautiful must something be if staring and praising is all you *want to do*? What if you imagine those angels not as horribly bored but inexpressibly, undistractably happy?

When have you been so absorbed by something that you couldn't possibly be distracted from it? I don't know what would make your list, but I've experienced that for the last few pages of a brilliant novel. I've been absorbed like that watching fourth-and-goal with the game on the line. Or looking into a sunset from the top of north Georgia's Blood Mountain. Or enjoying a fine meal with dear friends. I still remember feeling that way as I watched my wife walk down the aisle on our wedding day.

I don't know what's on your list, but I'll say this about mine: if I can't be distracted, I'm probably delighted. I'm certainly not bored.

What will seeing God be like for us? For all we don't know, it is safe to say that we will be completely absorbed by a beauty of which all other beauty anywhere else on earth is just the faintest shadow. I love how Jonathan Edwards puts it:

> To go to heaven, fully to enjoy God, is infinitely better than the most pleasant accommodations here. Fathers and mothers, husbands, wives, or children, or the company of earthly friends, are but shadows; but the enjoyment of God is the substance. These are but scattered beams; but God is the sun. These are but streams; but God is the fountain. These are but drops; but God is the ocean.[1]

Here is Edwards again: "After they have had the pleasure of beholding the face of God millions of ages, it will not grow a dull story; the relish of this delight will be as exquisite as ever."[2]

When we see God, we will necessarily, inevitably, joyfully, and *rightly* love what is most lovely. Which leads me to the second part of what John says.

What Will Seeing God Do to Us?

John's emphasis in 1 John 3:2 isn't primarily on what seeing God as he is will be like for us, but on what seeing God will do to us. "When he appears we shall be like him, because we shall see him as he is." Seeing him as he is will transform who we are. When we look at him, we will be like him. That is John's main point in this verse.

---

1 Jonathan Edwards, "The Christian Pilgrim, or, The True Christian's Life a Journey towards Heaven," in *The Works of Jonathan Edwards*, vol. 2 (1834; repr., Carlisle, PA: Banner of Truth, 1974), 244.

2 Jonathan Edwards, "The Pure in Heart Blessed," in *The Works of Jonathan Edwards*, vol. 2 (1834; repr., Carlisle, PA: Banner of Truth, 1974), 909.

But why? What is the connection between seeing God as he is and becoming like God ourselves? Why does looking at God produce likeness to God? Because in heaven, when we look on God as he is, we will so love what we see that the beauty of his holiness will make us holy too. We will be drawn into his holiness like a tractor beam, renovated from the inside out by the force of attraction.

I learned early on as a preacher that when I'm working on a sermon, I have to be really careful who I'm listening to and when I'm listening to them. Some preachers help me because we're so different. I would never think to break things down the way they do, ask the questions they ask, or draw out applications they recognize. With preachers like that I'm able to pick and choose what will work for me from a wide buffet of options I wouldn't have considered before. But there are other preachers who, for one reason or another, I just resonate with completely. If I listen to one of them too early in my preparation, I won't be able to shake the effect, and my sermon will just flow into what they said and how they said it. The effect is magnetic and irresistible.

Seeing God will have this effect on all God's children. We will be drawn to his beauty and shaped by his image, as naturally and irresistibly as water runs downhill. The link between looking and likeness is love.

This connection between love for God and obedience to God is all over 1 John. But this theme is important to John because it was important to Jesus and central to the entire Bible. When Jesus was asked to name the greatest commandment (Matt. 22:37; Luke 10:27), he named the command to love the Lord your God with all your heart, soul, mind, and strength (Deut. 6:5). The whole law flows from this fundamental command. You won't obey all God's other commands unless you love him. The commands are like varied expressions of love for him, put to action. And you can't disobey his other commands unless you love something else *more* than you love him.

The Bible often connects sin to the underlying problem of idolatry. With sin, just as with holiness, we become like what we see and love most. In *We Become What We Worship*, Bible scholar G. K. Beale traces the theme of idolatry across the Old and New Testaments and sums up the point in a sentence used throughout his book: "What people revere, they resemble, either for ruin or restoration."[3] We naturally conform our lives to whatever we love and trust above all. When that is anything belonging to this world—any creature loved apart from the Creator—we bring all sorts of ruin, large and small, both to ourselves and those around us. But the process works the other way around too. We are restored as we revere the one true God in all his beauty. Looking at him, we love him, and loving him, we come to be more like him.

For now, our hearts are the battleground for competing loves. Part of the torment of life in this world is the weakness of our love for God and the ease with which our heads can be turned toward one false hope and empty pleasure after another. We are so relentlessly gullible, let down at every turn, and disappointed most of all in ourselves. We know we ought to know better. That's why Paul's words are so relatable:

> For I do not understand my own actions. For I do not do what I want, but I do the very thing I hate. . . . For I do not do the good I want, but the evil I do not want is what I keep on doing. . . . For I delight in the law of God, in my inner being, but I see

3   G. K. Beale, *We Become What We Worship: A Biblical Theology of Idolatry* (Downers Grove, IL: InterVarsity Press, 2008), 16.

in my members another law waging war against the law of my mind and making me captive to the law of sin that dwells in my members. (Rom. 7:15, 19, 22–23)

If you can relate to his struggle, you can relate to his pleading, searching question: "Who will deliver me from this body of death?" (7:24).

The peace we crave will come only when we see God as he is. To long for heaven is to long for the "cessation of this war," as Augustine puts it. "We burn for entrance on that well-ordered peace in which whatever is inferior is forever subordinated to what is above it."[4] When he appears the war will be over.

For now, sin in our lives flows from idolatry in our hearts. We disobey God because we love something or someone else more. Heaven will mean the end of sin's power in our lives precisely because no one can see God as he is and worship any of his competition. When we see him face-to-face, nothing will ever turn our heads again. We will, finally and forever, love him with all our heart, soul, mind, and strength. As Augustine says of that day, "Purified and molten by the fire of your love, I flow together to merge into you."[5] We will be perfectly unified in love for the one who is perfectly lovely.

Purified by Hope on Earth

John turns from what will be in the future, when God appears, to what is happening now in the meantime: "Everyone who thus hopes

---

4   Quoted in Jerry Walls, *Heaven: The Logic of Eternal Joy* (New York: Oxford University Press, 2002), 37.

5   Saint Augustine, *Confessions*, trans. Henry Chadwick (Oxford: Oxford University Press, 1998), 244.

in him purifies himself as he is pure" (1 John 3:3). Hope for what you will be when you see him can purify you now while you wait.

This connection is not unique to John. Peter says basically the same thing in 1 Peter 1:13–16:

> Therefore, preparing your minds for action, and being sober-minded, *set your hope fully* on the grace that will be brought to you at the revelation of Jesus Christ. As obedient children, do not be conformed to the passions of your former ignorance, but as he who called you is holy, you also *be holy in all your conduct*, since it is written, "You shall be holy, for I am holy."

So does Paul in Colossians 3:2–5:

> *Set your minds on things that are above*, not on things that are on earth. For you have died, and your life is hidden with Christ in God. When Christ who is your life appears, then you also will appear with him in glory.
> *Put to death therefore what is earthly in you.*

It's as if Paul is saying, "Think on where you're going, then go ahead and dress appropriately."

If you're not cultivating focus on that day, if the hope of seeing God isn't controlling what you see around you here and now, your head will be turned again and again by the fool's gold of this world. As Richard Baxter puts it, "If the mind is either idle or ill-employed, the devil does not need a greater advantage. If he finds the mind empty, there is room for anything he wants to bring in." But the opposite also holds true: "A net or bait that is laid on the ground is unlikely to catch the bird that flies in the air; while she keeps above, she is out of the danger, and the higher she is, the safer she is. So it is with us."[6] Baxter is simply agreeing with John: "Everyone who thus hopes in him purifies himself as he is pure."

So how does this work out in practice? How does hope in the promise of perfect holiness in God's presence purify us now in the meantime? I see at least two factors. What we're hoping for shows us *how to fight for holiness* and *why the fight is worth it.*

How to Fight for Holiness

Looking, loving, likeness. That's how we'll be perfected in heaven. We grow in holiness as we grow in the knowledge and love of the Lord. To see him (knowledge) is to love him, and loving him leads to obeying him. So focus on the top of the chain. Every day, knock over that first domino. Look at what you will look at where you can already see it. Focus your mind on the one whose beauty will make you beautiful.

If looking leads to loving and loving leads to likeness, where should we look for God's beauty now, while we wait to see him face-to-face? He has made himself visible in the world all around us; we should learn to see him in every good thing we enjoy. He has made himself more visible in what he's told us about himself in his word, so all of it is useful to look at. Bible study is spiritual warfare. But if you want to see God now, while we wait to see him as he is, the best place to look is where he has shown us his love for us—in Christ.

John points the way: "See [or Behold! Look!] what kind of love the Father has given to us, that we should be called children of God; and so we are" (1 John 3:1). God loves his people as a father

---

6 Richard Baxter, *The Saints' Everlasting Rest*, updated and abridged by Tim Cooper (Wheaton, IL: Crossway, 2022), 97–98.

loves his children. But it was not easy for God to adopt us into his family. The love John has in mind is the love he wrote of in 4:7–10:

> Beloved, let us love one another, for love is from God, and whoever loves has been born of God and knows God. Anyone who does not love does not know God, because God is love. In this the love of God was made manifest among us, that God sent his only Son into the world, so that we might live through him. In this is love, not that we have loved God but that he loved us and sent his Son to be the propitiation for our sins.

When John says, "In this the love of God was made manifest among us," he's saying, "Here is some transforming, captivating, absorbing, and heavenly beauty you can already see right here and right now. Look at him laying down his life to bring life to the dead, to turn enemies into children. Look what it cost him, but more than that—look what he was willing to pay." And when you do, John shows what will happen. You'll love like he loves.

To fight for holiness, you need more than willpower. You need love. You need what Thomas Chalmers called "the expulsive power of a new affection."[7] Why would you give up one thing for another when you want the thing you already have? Only because you want the other thing more. And how do you come to want the other thing more? Only by looking closely at its beauty. To experience the expulsive power of a new affection, you need to look at him loving you.

John also tells us what this life-giving, sin-bearing, child-adopting love of God is aiming for in the lives of those he saves: "You

---

7 Thomas Chalmers, *The Expulsive Power of a New Affection* (1819; repr., Wheaton, IL: Crossway, 2020).

know that he appeared in order to take away sins. . . . The reason the Son of God appeared was to destroy the works of the devil" (1 John 3:5, 8).

Christ came for war against the one who has from the beginning been working to draw God's people away from God's promises, luring them with lies of goodness apart from God. He came to address the power of sin, not just its penalty, from the power of the evil one to the power of evil in each one of our hearts.

In our culture, we often associate love with the affirmation of whatever already is. You love others when you're happy with them just as they are. But God's love is deeper than that and aims to carry us further. The holiness that glorifies him is good for us. His love seeks our good through his glory.

His love, in other words, isn't just self-sacrificing. It is purpose driven. His love creates and cultivates. He loved into being a world that did not yet exist. He loved enemies into his family as his children. And when Christ gave himself on the cross, his aim was to love sinners into a loveliness we could never achieve apart from his love. He poured himself out to purify us from sin. We can't look at what it cost him to love us and remain casual about the sin in our lives that he came to destroy.

When my grandfather was a child, he lost his father to tuberculosis. It fell to his mother to provide for their large family through the depths of the Great Depression. In those lean years they barely had enough to survive on. One story from that period always broke my heart. Once his mother saved up enough money to send my grandfather down the street for an ice cream cone. This could not have been easy for her to manage. It surely meant sacrifice for her. Even more than that, it showed incredible love for him. As he was walking home from the drugstore, somehow he stumbled, lost his hold on the cone, and dropped it onto the filthy Jacksonville pavement, where that precious ice cream melted away. My grandfather told this story as a tragedy. He didn't mean to squander that gift of love and sacrifice. But what if he had dropped it on purpose? That would mean one of two things: either he lost sight of what this cost his mother, or he didn't care much about her in the first place.

We can't be casual about sin if we're clear on what our sin cost our Savior. We won't be casual about holiness if we see how important it is to the one who loves us so well. When we look on him, through the love he has already shown us—when we look at how far his love has gone to save us and at how committed he is to make us beautiful as he is beautiful—we love him more and more, and his objectives become ours. We want more and more what he wants for us because he wants it. And how could we shrug our shoulders at something he hates with such pure, passionate hatred? To shrug our shoulders at sin would be like shrugging our shoulders at him. "No one who abides in him keeps on sinning; no one who keeps on sinning has either seen him or known him" (1 John 3:6).

Why the Fight Is Worth It

The reality of the meantime is that the more we grow as Christians—the closer we get to him, the more pure we become—the more our ongoing sin will bother us. We will see our sin like he does, and our hatred for what he hates will grow with our love for him. The more sin we see, the more we will hate our sin, and the more reason we'll have for discouragement, if not for despair. How do we keep going when we see so much sin in ourselves? Only if we remember where all this is headed. Only if we know how this ends.

All John's confidence for our ultimate purification is rooted in the one who will finish the job. That confidence oozes through every phrase in our passage. We *are* God's children now. That's certain. *When*, not if, he appears. We *shall*, not might, be like him. Because we *shall* see him as he is. It's only a matter of time. And everyone who thus hopes *in him* purifies himself as he is pure. We know how this ends because our holiness is his personal project. And what he begins, he carries on to completion every time.

I love the way the apostle Paul drives home this same point in Titus 2:11–14:

> For the grace of God has appeared, bringing salvation for all people, training us to renounce ungodliness and worldly passions, and to live self-controlled, upright, and godly lives in the present age, waiting for our blessed hope, the appearing of the glory of our great God and Savior Jesus Christ, who gave himself for us to redeem us from all lawlessness and to purify for himself a people for his own possession who are zealous for good works.

Like John, Paul is placing our growth in holiness on a timeline, looking back to what God has already done, looking ahead to what will be when Christ returns, and in that light looking at what God is doing in his children right now, in the meantime. His grace has already appeared, when the Word became flesh. Now that grace is training us, like a parent trains up a child, to "live . . . godly lives in the present age" (Titus 2:12). And Paul makes it plain whose power this renovation project depends on and where all this is headed: Jesus "gave himself for us . . . to purify . . . a people for his own possession who are zealous for good works" (2:14). Jesus gave himself then so he could go on with his work of grace now, bringing goodness and beauty out of our lives. He will finish what he started because we belong to him.

Over the last ten years or so, my wife has developed a passion for gardening, and not just a passion but an obvious and wonderful skill for that work. She transformed our previous home's flower beds into a botanical wonderland with incredible variety and something for every season, with barely any space that wasn't used for beauty. Several years ago, after our church moved to a new and more permanent location, our family had the chance to move into a home a couple of blocks from our church building. This was an incredible opportunity and a wonderful gift from God. But let me tell you, it was not easy to leave those flower beds. In our new place, the garden space is what you might call a blank canvas. That would be the positive spin. Desert waste would perhaps be more realistic. Even several years in, compared to what she had before, these flower beds still have a long way to go. They don't have much to recommend them.

But the best thing about these beds—the most important thing to know about them—is that they belong to her now. She bought them at great cost. And now, in a way, she has given herself to purify them. It's a good thing to be a flower bed loved by this woman. She knows exactly what these plants need to stay healthy and strong. She pays constant, careful attention to them and knows how they're doing. She knows how to spot their enemies too and exactly how to fight them off. Their enemies are her enemies. And their flourishing is her passion.

When Paul talks of these upright, godly lives in the present age, of a people zealous for good works, he's not speaking these words behind a wagging finger with an "or else" following close behind. He's not speaking the language of threat but of promise. If you're in Christ, he's describing your future. You may not be much to look at now, but you are not yet what he will make you to be. You will be zealous for good works. You will thrive because his plants always do.

Maybe for you the ongoing battle with indwelling sin feels absolutely hopeless. If you had a God who was standing by, waiting to see how far you can go, it would be. You might as well give up now and save yourself the trouble. But that is not the sort of God you have. Christ has died, but Christ is risen. And he has been crystal clear about what he is doing with his life now. He is purifying for himself a people. He is purifying you.

Richard Sibbes puts it like this in *The Bruised Reed*:

> Christ will . . . take our part against our corruptions. They are his enemies as well as ours. . . . Let us not look so much at who our enemies are as at who our judge and captain is, nor at what they threaten, but at what he promises. We have more for us than against us. What coward would not fight when he is sure of victory? None is here overcome but he that will not fight.[8]

The one who began a good work in you will carry it on all the way to completion. He will carry you home, to see him face-to-face. And when you see him, you will be like him. So by all means, fight on. We know how this ends.

---

8   Richard Sibbes, *The Bruised Reed* (1630; repr., Carlisle, PA: Banner of Truth, 1998), 122.

4

Bound for Untouchable Security

How the Hope of Heaven Relieves
Our Anxiety in the Meantime

JESUS MADE MANY BOLD STATEMENTS, but I don't know if he made any statement that seems more radical or more impossible than the command of Matthew 6:25: "Do not be anxious about your life."

You probably don't need me to tell you that anxiety is a massive problem in our culture right now.[1] Perhaps you've seen mind-boggling statistics about the rising number of adults who report debilitating symptoms or the even more stunning rise of anxiety among kids and teens around the world. Perhaps you've heard people refer to what we're seeing as an anxiety epidemic. But whatever you may have observed in our culture, you probably don't need me to tell you that anxiety is a problem because when we're talking

---

1   My favorite recent descriptions of this cultural phenomenon especially among younger generations are from Jean Twenge, *Generations: The Real Differences between Gen Z, Millennials, Gen X, Boomers, and Silents—and What They Mean for America's Future* (New York: Atria, 2023); and Jonathan Haidt, *The Anxious Generation: How the Great Rewiring of Childhood Is Causing an Epidemic of Mental Illness* (New York: Penguin, 2024).

about anxiety, we're not just tracing stats and trends we can chart on a graph. We're talking about your life.

I know plenty of people who struggle greatly with anxiety. I don't know anyone who enjoys it or who wouldn't love to obey Jesus's command to not be anxious about life. More often than not anxiety feels like something that's happening to you, not something you're seeking out for yourself. You feel carried away by it, a victim of it, not someone who needs to be told to stop it. It's frustrating and sometimes it feels hopeless. That hopelessness is where I want to focus an attack in this chapter.

I've seen enough anxiety to know there's always more going on than I can see, from the mysteries of brain chemistry, to the impact of awful experiences, to the way you were raised, and no telling what else. My main goal is not to fully explain your experience of anxiety, much less to explain it away. I do want to show you what to do with it. Whatever may factor into the anxiety you experience, I want to demonstrate the hope of heaven as a powerful, underutilized weapon in the fight for peace. I want to show you how to fight back against anxiety with a cultivated focus on a different future than the possible future that's stressing you out.

There is no true peace without hope and no true hope without heaven. We need to know that what defines our future is an inheritance kept in heaven for us by a God who's keeping us for heaven. That is precisely the hope Peter holds out to us in 1 Peter 1:3–5. But first, I want to lay the groundwork for the perspective of heaven with a closer look at what is going on in our minds and hearts when we're anxious.

Understanding Anxiety

Some find it helpful to contrast anxiety with fear. Fear and anxiety share many of the same symptoms and cause the same reactions.

But fear is focused on a present threat, something right in front of you, like a rattlesnake slithering on the trail. Anxiety is focused on a possible threat. Fear focuses on what *is* happening. Anxiety focuses on what *might* happen. Fear goes as easily as it comes, once the snake slithers away into the brush. Anxiety is far more slippery, far more diffuse, far more difficult to get behind you.

Consider a few definitions of anxiety. The American Psychological Association defines anxiety as a "*future-oriented*, long-acting response broadly focused on a diffuse threat."[2] The American Psychiatric Association says "Anxiety refers to *anticipation of a future concern*."[3] And here is perhaps the most helpful definition I've seen: "Anxiety is both a mental and physical state of negative expectation. . . . Anxiety is meant to capture attention and stimulate you to make necessary changes to protect what you care about. . . . *Anxiety can be considered the price we humans pay for having the ability to imagine the future.*"[4]

Whatever else may contribute to our feelings, anxiety is an orientation toward the future. And underneath that orientation, we will find two basic assumptions that work together to make us miserable: my future is vulnerable, and my future is up to me.

Our Future Is Vulnerable

Several hundred years ago French philosopher Blaise Pascal gave one of my favorite descriptions of what it is to be human. He described us as thinking reeds.[5] A reed is vulnerable. It can be

2   "Anxiety," American Psychological Association, https://www.apa.org/. Emphasis mine.
3   "What Are Anxiety Disorders?," American Psychiatric Association, https://www.psychiatry .org/. Emphasis mine.
4   "What Is Anxiety?," *Psychology Today*, https://www.psychologytoday.com/. Emphasis mine.
5   Pascal, Number 200, in *Christianity for Modern Pagans: Pascal's* Pensees, ed. Peter Kreeft (San Francisco: Ignatius, 1993), 55.

trampled, scorched by sun, starved by lack of rain, eaten by bugs or animals, or burned by fire. And it's only a matter of time before summer turns to fall, fall turns to winter, and so the reed dies with the season. Humans are vulnerable too. A single drop of water can kill us, Pascal noticed, if it comes with the right contamination. And under the best possible circumstances, the Bible says that we are all of us like grass of the field (Isa. 40:6–8; 1 Pet. 1:24–25). We grow and thrive for a moment. We wither and fade over time.

But our glory and our misery is that we have to think about it. We're *thinking* reeds. It's tough to live in a world full of dangers as a reed who knows its vulnerability. We live in a world where stock markets crash. So do cars at high speeds. Tornadoes form up and drop down out of nowhere. Housing markets fluctuate. Jobs get downsized. Kids drown in swimming pools. As effective as medical care has become at protecting us and at putting us back together, the goalposts just keep moving. Early Americans worried about smallpox. My grandparents worried about tuberculosis and polio. Those problems are distant memories now, but nearly half of us will get cancer at some point. And when, Lord willing, we figure out a cure for this disease, some other killer will rise up to take its place. Our lives in this world are as vulnerable as ever. And Pascal was mostly thinking about our vulnerable bodies, but we could add to that the vulnerability of our relationships, social status, and all the adjacent anxieties unleashed in the age of social media. There are so many ways our lives could be upended, so many possibilities we want to avoid. As humans, we're stuck with the ability to know this about ourselves and to feel it in advance.

Our Future Is Up to Us

A second assumption combines with the first to make up a miserably bitter cocktail. It's not just that we know we're vulnerable, with an ability to imagine the future and all the things we'd like to avoid. We also tend to feel responsible for those uncertain futures and never more so than in the modern world.

According to Hartmut Rosa, for the last three hundred years Western culture has been driven by the goal of "relentlessly expanding humanity's reach." We moderns have what he calls an "aggressive relationship to the world."[6] By instinct, we try to bring as much of the world under our control as possible so that we can optimize our experience of it wherever possible.

You can now wear a watch that measures everything from your heart rate to the number of steps you've taken in a given day or week. It will track these metrics and display them for you with measurable results you can use to optimize your performance from one day to another and compare them with where you've been and where you want to be.

You can buy a grill that lets you set the temperature you want, monitor the temperature of your meat, and make adjustments on the fly all from an app on your phone, whether you're sitting on the couch or across town running errands. It's wild how much of our lives is customizable.

But the truth is that no one can customize the future. And the more you expect to customize, the more bothered you are by what you can't. Rosa cites research showing that the more security cameras, burglar alarms, and protective fencing people install, the less secure they feel. He writes, "The lack of effective individual control over something potentially controllable evidently transforms uncontrollability into powerlessness and insecurity."[7] In other words, the more you think you should be able to control,

6   Hartmut Rosa, *The Uncontrollability of the World* (Cambridge, UK: Polity, 2020), 8.
7   Rosa, *Uncontrollability*, 64.

the more you're burdened by what you can't control. The allure of more and more influence over your future creates an illusion that complete control is possible. And if you could control your future, you should control your future. We know and influence just enough to be miserable.

Everywhere we turn in this modern, secular age we're offered the freedom to build our lives on our terms. We're told to decide what to be and go be it. We're told to remember we've got what it takes, that we're strong enough, brave enough, and smart enough to grab life by the horns and go where we want to go. But in our hearts, in our chests, in our lungs, and in our shoulders we know better. When we push back on anxiety by looking at all we bring to the table, we are feeding the very problem we hope to solve.

There are any number of books, movies, podcasts, and influencers who will tell you the future is up to you and believe they're doing you a favor. But behind that glistening smile and all that positive energy is a truly terrifying prospect. "The future is up to you" is just another way of saying, "You're on your own."

In a way, anxiety is a form of loneliness—the inevitable lot of the thinking reed who's all alone. If this world is everything, and if it's on us to make the most of it, anxiety really does make sense. And I don't know of any way to get past it—unless this world is not everything, and we're not on our own after all. I don't know any way to get past it without the hope of heaven.

Looking to Heaven

First Peter 1:3–5 offers one of my favorite summaries of the hope of heaven. And at the core of what it celebrates are two pillars to our hope that are perfectly matched to the two major factors in our anxiety. On earth we are vulnerable, but our inheritance in heaven is not. We're tempted to feel responsible, but our lives are guarded by God. Peter writes,

> Blessed be the God and Father of our Lord Jesus Christ! According to his great mercy, he has caused us to be born again to a living hope through the resurrection of Jesus Christ from the dead, to an inheritance that is imperishable, undefiled, and unfading, kept in heaven for you, who by God's power are being guarded through faith for a salvation ready to be revealed in the last time. (1 Pet. 1:3–5)

Peter shows us the two most important things to know facing the future.

Our Inheritance Is Kept in Heaven,
So Our Future Is Not Vulnerable

Peter is overflowing with praise for God. He may as well be shouting from the page. And he quickly tells us why. God by his mercy has caused us to be born again to a living hope through the resurrection of Jesus from the dead. God has given us new birth into a new family, with a new citizenship and a new identity defined by the hope that Jesus was really dead but really came to life again.

What is this hope that makes us new, this hope that depends on him being alive again? Peter attempts to put words to it in 1:4. And the best he can come up with to describe this inheritance we're born into is a series of words that tell us what it's *not*.

This inheritance is *imperishable*. In this world every good thing is vulnerable. In heaven nothing dies.

This inheritance is *undefiled*. In this world every good thing comes tainted. More often than not, it is tainted by me—by my greedy desire for more, my preoccupation with what others have that I don't, my unrealistic expectations, or simply by my knowledge that no good thing lasts forever. In heaven all joy is pure.

This inheritance is *unfading*. In this world every good thing eventually ends. It's not just that it's perishable—that it could be destroyed. It's that it will be, eventually, lost to time. We tend mostly to fear what can be lost in a moment. But time brings a kind of slow-motion trauma that amounts to the same thing. On earth, everyone loses everything eventually. But not in heaven. There, no joy ever fades.

It's as if Peter is screaming at us, "THIS WORLD IS NOT EVERY-THING!" Another world is coming because Jesus came out of his grave. And that world, where our inheritance is kept, is a world of untouchable security.

It's also as if Peter is simply passing on the message of Jesus he heard from the master teacher in the Sermon on the Mount. Jesus said, "Do not lay up for yourselves treasures on earth, where moth and rust destroy and where thieves break in and steal" (Matt. 6:19). On earth, everything is vulnerable. Whatever we love can be lost in a moment, and sooner or later it will be lost to moth or rust. When our hearts are attached to what can't be protected, we have reason to be anxious. But Jesus also said, "But lay up for yourselves treasures in heaven, where neither moth nor rust destroys and where thieves do not break in and steal. For where your treasure is, there your heart will be also" (6:20–21). To have any peace, we need a treasure that can't be touched. That's what God is keeping for us in heaven.

With good reason, Revelation 21 pictures this new world as a new Jerusalem and gives detail upon detail about the walls that surround this happy place. To us that may seem a little anticlimactic, but in the ancient world there was no better way to picture security than with city walls. All those ancient stone walls all over Europe and Asia weren't built to look pretty or for the pleasure of future tourists. They were built because back then there was always someone out to get you and no way to feel safe but to live behind such walls. Heaven is a walled city. Nothing can get to what God has prepared for his people in that place. And that's why, in the words of Revelation 21:4, it is a world where "death shall be no more, neither shall there be mourning, nor crying, nor pain anymore, for the former things have passed away."

How can we have peace when we know that we are vulnerable? Only if we know this world is not everything. A new world is coming where nothing is vulnerable. And we have an inheritance in that world, kept in heaven for us. This is our future when we're born again to a living hope.

We Are Kept for Heaven, So Our Future Is Not Up to Us

In 1 Peter 1:5, Peter points to the second pillar of hope. It's not just that there is an inheritance kept in heaven for us, invulnerable to loss, change, decay, or anything. It's that we are being kept for heaven by God's power and not ours. On our own we would be vulnerable. But we are not responsible for our future. God is: "By God's power [we] are being guarded through faith for a salvation ready to be revealed in the last time."

Peter is once again looking to the future. He's speaking of a salvation not yet visible to us, ready to be revealed in the last time. But whether we get there depends upon God from beginning to end. God's mercy started all this (1:3), giving us new life, a new family, and a new hope of an inheritance. God's power raised Jesus from the dead (1:3). God keeps the inheritance secure beyond all threat (1:4). And God guards every one of his children all the way home (1:5). God is the golden thread binding this wonderful package together.

We are anxious when we feel responsible, as if all the outcomes depend upon us. But God is responsible for this future. Everything depends on him.

Once again, Peter is simply echoing what he heard from Jesus in the Sermon on the Mount. Soon after Jesus said to lay up treasures in heaven, beyond the reach of time or evil, he said not to be anxious about your life. But there, his focus was squarely on the God who is your Father and loves you too much to leave you on your own:

> Look at the birds of the air: they neither sow nor reap nor gather into barns, and yet your heavenly Father feeds them. Are you not of more value than they? And which of you by being anxious can add a single hour to his span of life? And why are you anxious about clothing? Consider the lilies of the field, how they grow: they neither toil nor spin, yet I tell you, even Solomon in all his glory was not arrayed like one of these. But if God so clothes the grass of the field, which today is alive and tomorrow is thrown into the oven, will he not much more clothe you, O you of little faith? Therefore do not be anxious, saying, "What shall we eat?" or "What shall we drink?" or "What shall we wear?" For the Gentiles seek after all these things, and your heavenly Father knows that you need them all. But seek first the kingdom of God and his righteousness, and all these things will be added to you. (Matt. 6:26–33)

What Jesus says about God was as radical in his time as the command not to be anxious. When he refers to the Gentiles and their seeking after all the material things of life, he's talking about how ancient pagans related to the world. They saw this world as everything. They believed there were gods, but their gods belonged to this world and none of them ruled over all of it. Most important of all, none of these gods was paying attention to their lives unless they did something to get the gods' attention. As one historian sums it up, "A god or goddess might occasionally take a liking, or a loathing, to some particular mortal. . . . For the most part, though, the gods were out for themselves, so to speak. They were mostly indifferent to the joys and sorrows of all the Marcuses, Gaiuses, and Juliuses of this world."[8] As the pagans saw things, you may not be on your own in this world, but it's certainly up to you to make the most of it.

It's as if Jesus is saying, "Of course the Gentiles are anxious about their lives, what they will eat or wear, who they'll marry, how people see them, how far they'll climb. They think the future is up to them. If they don't grab life by the horns, no one else will do it for them. But you don't have to live like the Gentiles." Jesus anchors our future in the fatherly care of the God who loves us. "Look at how he feeds the birds. Look at how he clothes the grass of the field. Are you not of more value than they? Of course you are because he loves you. Your heavenly Father already knows what you need without you telling him, and he wants good for you without you paying him. He's your Father. Just seek his kingdom, and he'll take care of everything else."

Applying Hope

For now, we're still vulnerable, facing all sorts of short-term possibilities we can't possibly control. That means we're going to struggle

---

8 Steven Smith, *Pagans and Christians in the City: Culture Wars from the Tiber to the Potomac* (Grand Rapids, MI: Eerdmans, 2018), 184.

with anxiety for as long as we live, in one form or another. That just is what it is. We do have to live as thinking reeds. But we do *not* have to live like pagans. God has given us exactly the medicine we need in the hope of heaven—a future that is not vulnerable, guaranteed by a God who is responsible. The key is to figure out where to apply that medicine. I want to spend the rest of this chapter thinking about how to draw on the hope of heaven to relieve anxiety in the meantime.

When we feel anxious, we're expecting something negative for our future. That's what anxiety is. The hope of heaven gives us another perspective on our future. We have an inheritance to set our hearts on that nothing can possibly touch and a Father who will guard us for that day no matter what may come our way in the meantime. These are the pillars of our hope for the future. When we feel anxious, we should ask which pillar is wavering and shore it up with the truth of the gospel.

Here are two questions to help with diagnosis so we'll know where to apply this cure.

Are we more attached to what is possible than to what God has promised us? Sometimes feelings of anxiety can be a sign that we're too attached to what we *can* lose and not as attached to what we *can't*. Sometimes our anxiety is a sign that we have anchored our lives to a future God has not promised us.

For as long as we live in this world, we will live with seemingly endless short-term possibilities. Many of these will be worthwhile goals certainly worth hoping for and even working toward. It's possible, for example, that you'll get the job you're hoping for. It's possible you'll earn a good living. It's possible your house will never burn to the ground. It's possible you'll someday get married or have children. It's possible your kids may grow up healthy, well-behaved, and ready to head off to a college they can afford. It's possible you'll save enough money to retire on. It's possible your adult kids will always want you in their life. It's possible you may not get cancer, Alzheimer's disease, or a debilitating injury. As we live in this world we have to consider all sorts of what-might-bes, short-term possibilities that we hope will go one way and not another. Proverbs is full of wisdom for how to seek good outcomes and how to avoid bad ones.

But the Bible is also clear about the danger we face when we look ahead to all those short-term possibilities. We will be relentlessly tempted to give our hearts to our version of a best-case future rather than the ultimate future God has promised us. We will be tempted every day to lay up treasures on earth rather than weighing everything by our untouchable inheritance.

Anxiety can be a warning sign to guard us: Is my heart attached to what I know, intuitively, I can't provide or protect? Am I set on something vulnerable to moth, rust, or thieves? Do I need to open my hands and set my mind on heaven, where my inheritance is imperishable, undefiled, and unfading? And whatever we may find when we answer these questions, the God-given, Spirit-backed, resurrection-tested medicine we need will always be exactly the same: we must remember that we are born again to a living hope, to an inheritance that is imperishable, undefiled, and unfading, kept in heaven for us. We must lay up treasures in heaven, where moth and rust cannot destroy.

Do we believe our future matters to us more than it does to God? Often when we feel anxiety, we're feeling the pressure of responsibility. As if it's on me to provide or protect what I love, as if the difference between outcomes I want and those I don't ultimately rests on me. We know in our bones that's too much weight to carry. We don't always know what's best. We can't ever control the future. We only suffer more when we act like that's not true. But sometimes we lose sight of God's fatherly care and operate like the future is up to us.

It's all too easy to slip into this trap because we're so used to believing no one cares as much about our future as we do. It is no easy thing to trust someone when it's your life that is on the line.

John Updike captures this tension beautifully in a short story called "Trust Me," in which a middle-aged man reflects back on his life, what it means to ask someone for trust, and what it costs that person to give it. At one point the man recalls a time when he used a pair of needle-nosed pliers to adjust the unruly braces in his daughter's mouth:

> She had come to him in pain, a wire gouging the inside of her cheek. But then, with his clumsy fingers in her mouth, her eyes widened with fear of worse pain. He gaily accused her, You don't trust me. The gaiety of his voice revealed a crucial space, a gap between their situations: it would be his blunder, but her pain. Another's pain is not our own.[9]

He's getting at what he calls the "space of indifference"—the inevitable gap between someone who asks to be trusted and the one who has to do the trusting. It's not his mouth that's on the line. A slip of the hand and he feels a little remorse, maybe some embarrassment. But his daughter will have a bleeding wound in her mouth. He's just not in her position. There's a gap between their situations.

9   John Updike, "Trust Me," in *Trust Me: Short Stories by John Updike* (New York: Knopf, 1987), 7.

Surely you've been there. Surely there have been times—with a doctor, an advisor, a boss, or a potential client—when you felt your life hinged on what to the other person was a 9 a.m. appointment. That gap—that space of indifference—is a powerful barrier to trust.

That's why in our fight against anxiety, as we cling to the promise that God guards us for heaven, there's nothing more crucial to remember than that our Father did not spare his own Son but freely gave him up for us all. The God who promised us an inheritance of untouchable security put his own skin in the game. Our future matters to him as much as it does to us.

There is inexhaustible, anxiety-fighting power in the words of Romans 8. In the incarnation of Jesus, God has shattered the illusion that there's any space of indifference between us. When he became like us in every respect, the Son collapsed the gap between our situation and his. God didn't spare his own Son so that he could give us everything he has promised to give us. He would not have paid such a cost if he were not planning to guard us all the way to glory.

When Paul says that God did not spare his own Son, he's reminding us that Jesus went to the cross in our place. Whatever terrible outcomes we may imagine in our mind are not the worst things that could happen to us. The worst thing that could possibly happen would be for us to face the wrath of God for our sin against him and be separated forever from the light and the life of his love.

The worst thing that could happen to us happened to Jesus instead so that it would never happen to us.

Now nothing can separate us from his love. Lots of terrible things could still happen. Paul lists them off in Romans 8. Our range of short-term possibilities includes tribulation, distress, persecution, famine, nakedness, danger, or sword (8:35). Feel free to add to that list whatever kept you awake last night.

But everything we encounter comes to our lives, as John Newton put it, from "the hand which was once nailed to the cross for us."[10] And none of those things will be able to separate us from the love of God in Christ Jesus our Lord.

In other words, there is no future outcome, no matter how fearsome, in which God will not be with you. He is with you now. He will be with you forever. Your future is up to him.

Bound for No More Pain

How the Hope of Heaven Makes Our
Suffering Meaningful in the Meantime

HUMANS CRAVE MEANING. It's one of the most distinctive things about us. It's not enough for us to know what has happened or is happening. We need to know why and what for. What does it all mean? I ask that question all the time.

Philosopher Thomas Nagel chose this question as the title for a short book introducing the study of philosophy to nonphilosophers like me. The book ends with a chapter on the meaning of life in which Nagel says there isn't one. We can't help taking ourselves seriously, he admits. And we especially can't help looking for significance in our work. We hope to accomplish something that matters, something that will make our lives count, something that will last longer than we do. But all that striving amounts to a fool's errand:

Even if you produce a great work of literature which continues to be read thousands of years from now, eventually the solar system will cool or the universe will wind down or collapse, and all trace of your efforts will vanish. In any case, we can't hope for even a fraction of this sort of immortality. If there's any point at all to what we do, we have to find it within our own lives.[1]

In other words, forget about connecting your life to anything bigger than you are. There's nothing out there, no master narrative your life fits into, no storyteller weaving all things together. You're just here until you're not. And in the meantime, the only meaning that matters is the meaning you can make within your own life. "The trick is to keep your eyes on what's in front of you, and allow justifications to come to an end inside your life, and inside the lives of others to whom you are connected."[2]

There's a brutal sort of logic to what Nagel is saying. If, as he believes, there's no Creator and sustainer behind our universe, then our lives come from nowhere, they're going nowhere, and the best we can hope for is to decide what matters to us for these brief moments in which we're alive. It's a brutal thought, but there's a kind of consistency to it.

To me, the real question is whether anyone can possibly live like this over the long haul. Maybe keeping your eyes on what's in front of you works pretty well when you're in your twenties, with a good-paying job, a thick network of friends, lots of options for the weekend, and freedom to travel whenever you want to. There could be a window of time and circumstance in which a lack of larger meaning feels like freedom to do whatever you want.

1 Thomas Nagel, *What Does It All Mean? A Very Short Introduction to Philosophy* (New York: Oxford University Press, 1987), 96.
2 Nagel, *What Does It All Mean?*, 100.

But what about when you're keeping your eyes on what's in front of you, and everything you see within your own life looks absolutely terrible?

Psychologist and holocaust survivor Victor Frankl offers another perspective in his bestselling book *Man's Search for Meaning*, a powerful story with profound insight into human nature.[3] Frankl spent years in a Nazi concentration camp during World War II. Before the war, he had already distinguished himself as a psychologist and researcher. He took his keen analytical eye with him into the daily tortures of the camp and turned his excruciating experience into a research experiment. How do people respond when basically everything is taken away except their capacity for pain and suffering? Why did some break down under those conditions? How did others find the strength to push through? Frankl studied his own mind and heart. He studied the prisoners around him. And he wrote up his conclusions after the war in *Man's Search for Meaning*.

What did he find? On one hand, "the prisoner who had lost faith in the future—his future—was doomed. . . . Usually it began with the prisoner refusing one morning to get dressed and wash or to go out on the parade grounds. No entreaties, no blows, no threats had any effect. He just lay there, hardly moving. . . . He simply gave up."[4] Once a prisoner told Frankl he'd had a dream that he would be released on March 30, 1945. He got a fever on the twenty-ninth. He was not released on the thirtieth. On the thirty-first he was dead. On the surface it looked like typhus, but Frankl knew better: "The ultimate cause of my friend's death was that . . . he was severely disappointed."[5] Hopelessness is lethal.

3   Victor Frankl, *Man's Search for Meaning* (1946; repr., Boston: Beacon, 2006).
4   Frankl, *Man's Search*, 74.
5   Frankl, *Man's Search*, 75.

On the other hand, with hope we can carry on through anything. We just have to know what the suffering is *for*. We need some purpose that makes it worthwhile. For some in the camp, that was a child or a spouse waiting for them on the outside. For others it was work they desperately wanted to get back to. One way or another, as Frankl put it, when a person knows the *why* for his existence, he will be able to bear almost any *how*.

It's common for Christians, when we suffer, to wonder why God allows his people to go through so many terrible things. His word says he loves us. His word says he's powerful. His word says he knows the plans he has for us, and they're plans to prosper and not to harm us. If all this is true, why do we go through all that we go through? What is God doing?

This is the right question to ask. It's appropriate, wise, and better than the impulse to fix everything in sight.

The first time my oldest son tried out for his middle school track team, he didn't quite make the cut. It made sense why he didn't make it on his first try, especially since it wasn't something he had a history with. But it was also one of the first times he had tried out for something he wanted to do and didn't succeed. I hated watching him suffer through that disappointment.

Naturally, my response was to jump straight into fix-it mode. I tried to explain it in context. I reminded him he hadn't hit his growth spurt yet, so his stride was a lot shorter than most of the other kids. Keep working, I assured him, and it'll come. I talked to him about all the things we could do to get him ready for the next tryout. We would make up some summer training plans, he could run cross-country in the offseason, that sort of thing. I even tried spin: it's a good thing, really, because now you'll have more time to focus on your baseball season.

All of this was true. Maybe some of it was helpful. But the next time my wife and I were alone, I finally got around to asking her what she'd said to help him. She said she had simply asked him a question: Why do you think God allows his children to go through times of disappointment like this?

I drilled down on quick solutions for his situation. She drilled down on the bigger story his situation fit into.

I wanted to fix his problem. She wanted to fix his perspective on God, what he's doing, and where all this is going.

My approach basically amounted to "Don't lose heart buddy, we can fix this." Her approach: "Don't lose heart. God is working for your good."

This is the perspective we need. Sooner or later, in large ways and small, everybody suffers, and no one gets out of life alive. No matter how young and healthy we may be, no matter how successful we have been so far, no matter how well things may have fallen into place for us, as Tim Keller put it, we've all got a lot of death in our future.[6] Bodies break down. Relationships fall apart. Dreams fade out. Jobs come and go, and even the best are miserable sometimes. Everybody suffers in this world as it is now. We will too. And if we're going to carry on, we need to know what it all means. We need to know how what we're going through connects to where we're going.

The apostle Paul points the way in 2 Corinthians 4:16–18:

> So we do not lose heart. Though our outer self is wasting away, our inner self is being renewed day by day. For this light momentary affliction is preparing for us an eternal weight of glory

---

6 Tim Keller, "Death and the Christian Hope," April 4, 2004, *Gospel in Life*, https://podcast .gospelinlife.com/.

beyond all comparison, as we look not to the things that are seen but to the things that are unseen. For the things that are seen are transient, but the things that are unseen are eternal.

I would sum up Paul's insight like this: if you're going to carry on without losing heart, you need to know that heaven is where you are going, and suffering is how you will get there.

Paul frames these few verses with two statements. The first is about our frame of mind and heart now, in the *present*: we do not lose heart (4:16). The second is about our perspective on the *future*: we look not to the things we can see, which are transient, but to the things we can't see, which are eternal (4:18). When he talks about these unseen, eternal things, he has in mind the same hope he wrote about in 4:14: "He who raised the Lord Jesus will raise us also with Jesus and bring us with you into his presence." He has in mind what he talks about in the very next verses: "a building from God, a house not made with hands, eternal in the heavens" (5:1), where "what is mortal may be swallowed up by life" (5:4). He's talking about heaven—God's promised future for his precious people.

Paul doesn't lose heart because he has set his hope for heaven firmly and squarely in the center of his horizon. He knows the why for his existence and for everything he experiences along the way. That's why he keeps his eyes fixed on what is unseen and eternal. If we want to carry on, we have to follow his lead. We need to know that we are going to a place where what we love most we can't possibly lose, a place where there is no more pain to suffer through, and no more death in our future.

Keeping this focus on where we are going is so much easier said than done, especially when heaven is a place we *can't* see and there's so much obvious suffering in what we *can* see all around us. What a gift for us that between these two statements Paul makes one all-important connection to put our suffering in perspective. For us to avoid losing heart in this world as it is while we look toward the world to come, we need to understand how our present affliction connects to our heavenly future. Paul shows us two ways.

In Our Suffering, God Is Preparing Us for Heaven

Paul begins to make this connection in 2 Corinthians 4:16. We do not lose heart because though the outer man is passing away, the inner man is being renewed day by day. What is he talking about? How does this protect us from losing heart?

It's important to know what he doesn't mean. It sounds a bit like Paul is just spouting the Greek philosophy so popular in his time. The idea was that the true you is the soul that's trapped in your body. The goal is to minimize the impact of your body for now and eventually to get free of your body, like a nut coming out of its husk.

But Paul has something else in mind. We know that because he's just been talking about the hope of resurrection—not that we will escape our bodies, but that one day we will see them renewed and transformed just like Jesus's body (4:14). And he's about to say we don't want to be unclothed, as if our soul might shed this pitiful physical outerwear, but further clothed. We will never be less than what we are now, only more—unimaginably more.

When Paul contrasts the outer self with the inner self, he's talking about our lives in two different eras of the world that are now overlapping.[7] The distinction isn't between life in the body and the life of the soul. The distinction is between life in this present age,

---

7   For this interpretation and throughout the following paragraphs, I was helped by Mark Seifrid, *The Second Letter to the Corinthians*, Pillar New Testament Commentary (Grand Rapids, MI: Eerdmans, 2014), 215.

under the influence of sin, death, and all their terrible minions, and life in the age to come, which already began to break in when Jesus came out of his grave and sent his Spirit into the hearts of his people.

Right now, our lives belong to both ages. There's an outer self that we're still affected by—better to say afflicted by—every single day. The outer self is vulnerable to affliction of all sorts, from these bodies that break down over time to the joys that come and go with time. And underneath it all, the life of the outer man is not a renewable resource. It's got a fixed content, and we drain it down breath by breath, day by day. That's what Paul's talking about. We are wasting away.

But meanwhile, Paul says, our inner self—the self that belongs to the new world God has promised, the self that's looking more and more like Jesus—is being renewed day by day. I'm convinced what Paul means is not simply that God is renewing us despite the fact that we're wasting away. As in, "I know it's tough to be wasting away, but cheer up, at least over here you're being renewed. It's not all bad!" I believe he means us to see that God is renewing the inner man through the affliction of the outer man. It is as the outer man wastes away that the inner man is being renewed.

I believe Paul has something similar in mind to what he said a few verses earlier, in 2 Corinthians 4:7, about his weakness and how God uses it: "We have this treasure in jars of clay." But why? Why jars of clay, so fragile and unimpressive? Paul's answer: "To show that the surpassing power belongs to God and not to us." God keeps us weak to give us the joy of trusting in him and not ourselves. He wants us to know what we have in him. *Our* weakness is *his* strategy.

It is through our affliction, through the wasting away of the outer man, that God is showing us who we have in him. Heaven is defined by the joy of his presence. If we don't enjoy him here, we wouldn't enjoy him there. As the outer man gets stripped away, the inner man gets a stronger and clearer taste of heaven's joys—the goodness of knowing God for his own sake.

I started drinking coffee as a kid. My parents would let me have it once a week on Saturday mornings. Early on it was always stale grounds from a can, from who knows where, roasted who knows when, and always full of cream and sugar. Now I know better. Over the years I've had better and better coffee, and I've learned to taste the difference. My palate can't detect the notes of blueberry, citrus, chocolate, honey, or whatever else might be printed on the package. I can, however, taste the difference between mass-market stuff from a can and the fresh-ground, fresh-roasted beans I use at home. And I can taste the difference between what I brew at home and what I get at my favorite coffee shop near my house.

Crema Coffee Roasters is simply phenomenal, but it was an acquired taste. I first had to strip away the sugar bit by bit, then remove the cream, then improve the beans little by little. Over time I understood the difference between beans and how they are brewed. As a kid, Crema would have been lost on me at best, its glory veiled by a heavy dose of cream and sugar contamination. At worst, I would have hated it.

Our taste for heaven's joy is something like that. God himself is the essence of heaven's joy. He is what we will love best about where we are going. But for now his glory is veiled by the sin in our hearts and challenged by alluring competitors in the world around us. And we're always tempted to turn God into a means to some other end. To fully enjoy what heaven is going to be, we need to have our palates refined. We need to acquire a taste for who we have in him.

God does this work through affliction. As our outer self wastes away, as the cream and the sugar are lost to us little by little, the inner self—the self that loves God, that's headed for heaven, that's already tasting of its life through the Spirit because of the Son—that self is being renewed. And not in spite of the fact that the outer self is wasting away, but precisely because that outer self is wasting away.

This is how God has always worked in his people. Do you remember the purpose behind Job's suffering? Satan claimed that Job only worshiped the Lord because of all the Lord had given him (Job 1:6–12). It's as if he was saying to God, "Take away the cream and sugar and see how he likes you straight." But the Lord knew better. When he took everything from Job, he didn't do it to harm his righteous servant. He did it to show the evil one, and to show Job, that God himself is the greatest gift of all.

This is also the point of Psalm 73. The psalmist starts out admitting he used to envy the wicked. They seem to have everything they could want. They have plenty to eat. They have power, influence, and money. They have loads of fun and no pangs until death. Meanwhile, the psalmist keeps his heart clean and hands washed, and yet he's stricken all day and rebuked in the morning. In terms of this world, the psalmist feels like he's losing. But then the switch flips, and he realizes the prosperity of the wicked is a curse. Their ease, their lack of affliction, is blinding them. What looks so stable and rewarding now will be swept away in a moment, like a dream that ends when you wake up. Meanwhile, he has learned a powerful lesson in his affliction:

Nevertheless, I am continually with you;
   you hold my right hand.
You guide me with your counsel,

and afterward you will receive me to glory.
Whom have I in heaven but you?
And there is nothing on earth that I desire besides you.
My flesh and my heart may fail,
  but God is the strength of my heart and my portion
    forever. (Ps. 73:23–26)

So long as God is the coffee-flavored splash of Folgers in our cup of cream and sugar, we're not ready for Crema Coffee Roasters. But through our affliction, he is refining our palates for a deeper joy in him than we have known to long for. He is proving that he tastes delicious all by himself. He's teaching us to crave the good stuff, to say "there is nothing on earth that I desire besides you." And then, almost unbelievably, he's going to give it to us: "God is . . . my portion forever."

Through our affliction, as the outer self is wasting away, God is renewing the inner self day by day to prepare us for the joy of his presence. God is preparing us for heaven.

In Our Suffering, God Is Preparing Heaven for Us

It's a bit provocative to consider that in our suffering God is preparing heaven for us, but look at how Paul explains why we do not lose heart: "For this light momentary affliction is preparing for us an eternal weight of glory beyond all comparison" (2 Cor. 4:17). There is endless encouragement to face anything if we understand what Paul means in this verse.

I fear that if we aren't careful, when we read this verse from the midst of some affliction, we can be discouraged rather than encouraged by it. We can see Paul label our afflictions as light and momentary compared to the glory of heaven and assume he writes with a shrug of his shoulders. So what's the big deal? Why are we hurting so badly? Why can't we just get over it? Do we not want eternal glory? If we're not careful, we might add to our pain the shame of being bothered by it in the first place.

That's not at all what Paul wants us to do. He is not simply saying that this too shall pass, so keep calm and carry on. He knows better than to say something like that. And he's not speaking from the cheap seats like I would be if I were saying something like this. He knows what it is to suffer. Later on in this letter, he gives us a list of the afflictions he has in mind:

Five times I received at the hands of the Jews the forty lashes less one. Three times I was beaten with rods. Once I was stoned. Three times I was shipwrecked; a night and a day I was adrift at sea; on frequent journeys, in danger from rivers, danger from robbers, danger from my own people, danger from Gentiles, danger in the city, danger in the wilderness, danger at sea, danger from false brothers; in toil and hardship, through many a sleepless night, in hunger and thirst, often without food, in cold and exposure. And, apart from other things, there is the daily pressure on me of my anxiety for all the churches. (2 Cor. 11:24–28)

You get the sense that he could keep adding to this list. He's always honest about how hard his life has been. He doesn't minimize his affliction, and he wouldn't minimize ours either.

Paul is not saying our suffering is not significant. He's saying our suffering is productive and worthwhile. He's showing us what our suffering *means*.

The key is to look at the verb. Paul says, "This light momentary affliction *is preparing* for us an eternal weight of glory" (2 Cor.

4:17). Affliction prepares glory. This is what I mean when I say that in our suffering God is preparing heaven for us.

Of course, on one level, heaven is what heaven is. Defined by the presence of God, who doesn't change, heaven is wonderfully, gloriously, and eternally unchanging. Heaven is what heaven is. But what heaven is *to us* will be determined, in part, by the suffering we endure in the meantime. The contrast is what will open our eyes and our hearts to the beauty of that new world.

Think about it. Water is what water is. All things being equal, it has the same taste and the same nourishment all the time. But what water is to me is affected by whether I have just come in from a run. Every now and then when I'm pressed for time, I'll do hill repeats in my neighborhood on Ninth Street, between Fatherland Street and Boscobel Street. I hope it helps because it's absolutely miserable, especially in the heat of summer. After half an hour or so, I will shuffle home, stumble into my kitchen, grab a glass from the cabinet, fill it with ice, and drink down three or four glasses of water before I stop to breathe. There is nothing in all the world like that taste in that situation. Water is always wonderful. It's always better for us than anything else we could drink. But what it is *to me* is affected by affliction. Every step up that hill prepares the weight of glory in a glass of ice water.

This is what Paul has in mind when he says our affliction prepares glory. It's as if our future glory *feeds on* our present suffering, growing in size and substance, like a growing body feeds on good protein. Perhaps that is why Paul speaks a few verses later of "what is mortal [being] swallowed up by life" (2 Cor. 5:4), or elsewhere of death being "swallowed up in victory" (1 Cor. 15:54, alluding to Isa. 25:8). The glory of heaven is strengthened, even nourished, by our knowledge of what it replaces and redeems.

Richard Baxter was convinced that in heaven we will keep our memory of earth so that we can compare the past with our present and know how good we have it in God's presence. "To stand at that height where we can see the wilderness and Canaan both at once, to stand in heaven and look back on earth and weigh them together in the balance, how that must transport the soul!"[8] From that height, with the perspective of heaven, you will see that "your Lord intended sweeter ends than you would believe. Your Redeemer was saving you just as much when he crossed your desires as when he granted them, just as much when he broke your heart as when he bound it up."[9]

Surely Baxter was onto something. Surely this is why Revelation 21 describes the beauty of the New Jerusalem through the ugliness that will not be there. A city defined by *no more*: "And death shall be no more, neither shall there be mourning, nor crying, nor pain" (21:4). The joy of *no more* feeds on the tears that God will one day wipe away. The one seated on the throne says "*to the thirsty* I will give from the spring of the water of life without payment" (21:6).

Our suffering is making us thirsty. And that means it is producing something far more valuable for us than what it takes from us. The real cost of our afflictions may be high, but that cost cannot compare to the eternal weight of glory suffering is preparing for us.

Paul is not trying to minimize our suffering or somehow sweep it under the rug. He's showing us how what we're going through connects to where we're going. He's putting our suffering into the story where it belongs, as part of how God brings us all the way

---

8   Richard Baxter, *The Saints' Everlasting Rest*, updated and abridged by Tim Cooper (Wheaton, IL: Crossway, 2022), 37.
9   Baxter, *Saints' Everlasting Rest*, 38.

home. He's saying, "This trade works out for you. This is a steal of a deal for you. It's worth it. Don't lose heart."

You need to know the meaning of what you're facing because when you know the *why*, you can put up with any *how*. I won't pretend to know how you're hurting today, much less how you'll be hurting tomorrow. I have no reason and no desire to minimize, simplify, or explain away any of it. But I do want to assure you of this. Your suffering is no diversion. Your pain will not be wasted. Whatever else he may be doing in your life, with every pang and every tear, God is preparing you for heaven, and he is preparing heaven for you. You are headed for glory. Suffering is how you will get there. And, as John Newton put it, "When you get to heaven, you will not complain of the way by which the Lord brought you."[10]

---

10   Newton to the Rev. Mr. Whitford, July 29, 1761, in *The Letters of John Newton* (1869; repr., Carlisle, PA: Banner of Truth, 2007), 45. Newton reflected on this theme often in his letters. Another favorite example is from a letter on May 21, 1763 to Captain Alexander Clunie: "He who has been with us thus far, will be with us to the end. He knows how to manifest himself even here, to give more than he takes away, and to cause our consolations to exceed our greatest afflictions. And when we get safe home, we shall not complain that we have suffered too much in the way. We shall not say, Is this all I must expect after so much trouble? . . . One sight of Jesus as He is, will fill our hearts, and dry up all our tears. Let us then resign ourselves into his hands; let us gird up the loins of our minds, be sober and hope to the end" (59–60).

6

Bound for Endless Love

How the Hope of Heaven Makes Our
Grief Bearable in the Meantime

AFTERLIFE BY BRITISH ACTOR and writer Ricky Gervais is a comedy, but it may be the saddest show I've ever watched. Its title is a clever one, given the central question explored throughout the series: What is life after the death of one you love when you don't believe in an afterlife? The genius of the show captures what it looks like to grieve without hope in a secular culture where God is conspicuously absent.

The central character is a man named Tony, a middle-aged reporter in a quaint English village who has just lost his wife to cancer. He's coming to grips with her death in the age of the smartphone camera. Every day he's pulled back to the past, watching an endless stream of videos from the cloud where her sort-of presence onscreen highlights her absence from real life. This is what haunting looks like in the twenty-first century.

Meanwhile, his father lives on in a nearby nursing home, suffering from advanced dementia and struggling to remember his own son. If all those videos drag Tony back to the past, visits to his father show him his future. He has this to look forward to. For much of the show he is on the verge of ending his own life. If not for his dog—their dog—he probably would.

There's nothing in his work to dull his pain. He writes for a struggling paper barely anyone reads. Sure, there are glimmers of light in the care he receives from his quirky group of friends. There's plenty of charm in their small-town lives. But even in its lighthearted moments, this is a show about the hopelessness of irreversible loss.

Afterlife is a far cry from Christian programming, but it's a powerful backdrop for the message of the gospel. It is a terrible thing to grieve without hope. And because of Jesus, you don't have to. You do have to grieve. But you don't have to grieve without hope.

In this chapter I want to show how the hope of heaven makes grief bearable in the meantime, specifically grief over the death of fellow Christians that you love.[1] At the heart of what the Bible teaches about heaven is the promise that we will one day be reunited with all those who have died in faith to live in a world of endless love, where the pain of loss is felt and feared no more.

---

1   I am limiting my focus to grief and hope following the death of fellow believers, who have died in the hope of a final reunion in heaven. This leaves unanswered and obvious questions about those who die apart from Christ and how to deal with grief in that uniquely painful situation. Though the chapter doesn't branch into this topic, I want to mention two things. First, we must do everything we can to avoid that terrible outcome while there is still time. The reality of death apart from Christ grieves us because it is grievous. We must face up to that reality and let a holy fear drive us to do what we can to appeal to our unbelieving friends and family, no matter the cost that appeal may bring. And second, for those already grieving over loved ones who have died apart from faith in Christ, the right and only place to turn is to the God of all comfort. He is good. He only ever does what is right. And he has promised to one day remove and redeem all sorrow.

Why Grief Is Unavoidable

Before we get to that message of hope, we need to be honest about why we so badly need what God has promised in the first place. We have to understand why grief is unavoidable for all of us. I would sum it up like this: relationships are precious, no one lives forever, and there's nothing on earth to draw that sting.

Relationships Are Precious

The most meaningful things in life are relationships of love with other people. I don't care how introverted you are, how much you may like space, peace, and quiet, and whether you may think of yourself as an animal person instead of a people person. No matter who you are, you need love in your life.

In 2023, two researchers from Harvard published the results of the longest-running study of human life ever conducted in a book called *The Good Life*. The study began in 1938 with more than seven hundred original participants, and it's expanded since then to include thirteen hundred of their descendants, tracking not just their experiences but how they saw them, asking questions about what makes them happy and what doesn't. The one dominant finding in the study should come as no surprise: "Good relationships keep us healthier and happier. Period."[2]

It's just not debatable. All of us need people to love and be loved by. Of course I'm not mainly talking about romantic love, as wonderful as that can be. I'm talking about love in general—all relationships of mutual knowledge and care. Close friends. Faithful colleagues. Fishing buddies. Brothers and sisters. Parents and children. And yes, of course, husbands and wives.

2   Robert Waldinger and Marc Schulz, *The Good Life: Lessons from the World's Longest Scientific Study of Happiness* (New York: Simon & Schuster, 2023), 10.

There are plenty of things we enjoy about life, from work to travel to music to sports to good food. But we've seen it in countless books and movies, if not in lives playing out around us—those who sacrifice relationships for the sake of career or personal pleasures end up miserable and alone. They end up miserable *because* they end up alone.

On the other hand, there is nothing in life that correlates to happiness more strongly than meaningful relationships. The best thing about life is love.

No One Lives Forever

This is where things get painful. Sooner or later, everyone loses everyone they love. No one lives forever.

When someone dies, it's common for the living to focus on the cause of death. It might have been a traffic accident or a heart attack, an aneurysm out of nowhere, or an on-again, off-again battle with cancer. If we can name the cause, we can try to avoid it ourselves. We can fight back with all the resources we can muster. After all, of the seemingly infinite ways there are to die, nearly all of them aren't going to be a problem for me and my people. But the truth is everyone dies of something sooner or later.

The first time you lose someone close to you, you also lose a sort of innocence. Some people seem too precious not to be there. Their death can seem almost impossible. But there is nothing on earth more inevitable.

This awakening is what the *New Yorker* writer Kathryn Schulz experienced when her father died sooner than anyone had expected. As she puts it in her memoir, *Lost and Found*, our losses are profoundly disorienting "not because they defy reality but because they reveal it."[3] Loss is terribly normal. As surely as 2 + 2 = 4, grief flows from the combination of two simple facts: the best thing about life is love, and eventually everyone loses everyone. This painful equation forces us to confront what Schulz calls the "most enduring problem of love, which is also the most enduring problem of life": "how to live with the fact that we will lose it."[4]

This is the right question. How can we live with the fact that everyone loses everyone they love, and the more you love someone the more it hurts when you lose that person? Is there any way to draw the sting of death?

Nothing Can Draw the Sting

From what I can see, there are two common ways of making death more tolerable, and neither one of them really works.

First, we can rebrand death as life. Think of this as *The Lion King* option. Death is nothing to worry about because it's really just part of the circle of life. The antelope eats the grass. The lion eats the antelope. The grass eats the lion. Then the next antelope has plenty to eat before the next lion comes to eat him. We're all part of one big circle in which no one really dies. We just live on in the digestive systems of all that come after us.

The problem is that no one can live like this is true. We just know better. Even Simba knew better. When Mufasa was thrown from the cliff by his evil brother Scar, then trampled by the herd of stampeding water buffalo, Simba didn't comfort himself with the thought that now the antelope of tomorrow would have plenty of well-fertilized grass to feed on. He cried his eyes out like the rest of us because he didn't want his dad to be dead.

3   Kathryn Schulz, *Lost and Found: A Memoir* (New York: Random House, 2022), 19.
4   Schulz, *Lost and Found*, 228.

Death is not just one of those things. It's devastating. It's personal. And on earth, it's irreversible. There is no circle, just a brutally straight line. Life begins. Life ends. And the living go on living with the hole left behind.

Another option is to rebrand loss as gain. We could face up to the reality that nothing lasts forever and let that drive us to squeeze as much joy out of what we have for as long as we have it. This is the lemonade Schulz makes of life's lemons: "Loss, which seems only to take away, adds its own kind of necessary contribution. . . . Disappearance reminds us to notice, transience to cherish, fragility to defend. Loss is a kind of external conscience, urging us to make better use of our finite days."[5] In other words, accepting that nothing lasts makes life sweeter, richer, more acute and alive in the meantime.

Surely there is wisdom in this perspective for those of us whose loved ones are still living. It can deepen our gratitude. It can bring focus to our days, months, and years together while we have them. But let's be honest: there is precious little comfort here for the grieving, who have loved and lost and now long to go back. There may be some wisdom here, but there is no hope at all.

When you are faced with the death of someone you love, you need something more than false comforts like these. What you crave is the irreplaceable hope at the heart of Christianity.

Heaven Is a World of Love Stronger Than Death

Most people for most of history have believed in some form of life after death. But only the hope of the gospel speaks to our deepest longing, faced with the death of someone we love. We want more

5   Schulz, *Lost and Found*, 236.

than life after death. As Tim Keller put it, we want love after death.[6] In heaven, according to the Scriptures, that is what we will have. The hope of heaven is hope for personal reunion with all those who have died in faith, with relationships restored beyond the grip of the grave. And though this hope speaks to our deepest longings, it is not just wishful thinking. It is rooted in the personal resurrection of Jesus.

The best place to see this teaching about heaven is 1 Thessalonians 4:13–18, where Paul writes to Christians who are grieving over those they have lost:

> But we do not want you to be uninformed, brothers, about those who are asleep, that you may not grieve as others do who have no hope. For since we believe that Jesus died and rose again, even so, through Jesus, God will bring with him those who have fallen asleep. For this we declare to you by a word from the Lord, that we who are alive, who are left until the coming of the Lord, will not precede those who have fallen asleep. For the Lord himself will descend from heaven with a cry of command, with the voice of an archangel, and with the sound of the trumpet of God. And the dead in Christ will rise first. Then we who are alive, who are left, will be caught up together with them in the clouds to meet the Lord in the air, and so we will always be with the Lord. Therefore encourage one another with these words.

There are two things worth noticing about what Paul is doing in these verses. First, he is contrasting the Thessalonians' hope as Christians to what was available to others around them. Paul says they should grieve differently because they see the future differently.

---

6 Tim Keller, "Hopefulness," April 18, 2019, in *Questioning Christianity with Tim Keller*, podcast, https://qcpodcast.gospelinlife.com.

In the Greco-Roman world of Paul's letter, there were various options for understanding death and what comes after. But all the options available agreed about one thing: death is a fundamental, irreversible separation. On that point the pagans agreed with the Epicureans, who agreed with the Stoics and with everyone else. Perhaps the soul goes on to some shadowy underworld. Perhaps, if you lived well, you live on in the hearts or memories of those who come after you. But there is no coming back from the grave and no chance of further life as *you*—your body, your mind, your memory, your perspective, or your relationships.

For Paul's friends in Thessalonica, one of the most influential responses to the problem of death was the response of the Stoics. In *A Brief History of Thought*, philosopher Luc Ferry gives a helpful summary of the Stoic perspective but pinpoints its central unsatisfying flaw:

> The Stoic doctrine of salvation is resolutely *anonymous* and *impersonal*. It promises us eternity, certainly, but of a non-personal kind, as an oblivious fragment of the *cosmos*. . . . Stoicism tries valiantly to relieve us of the fears linked to death, but at the cost of obliterating our individual identity. What we would like above all is to be reunited with our loved ones, and, if possible, with their voices, their faces—not in the form of undifferentiated cosmic fragments, such as pebbles or vegetables.[7]

Without the promise of reunion, a Stoic could only ever grieve without hope. This was the gap into which Christian hope burst onto the scene, bringing an altogether new perspective on death

---

7   Luc Ferry, *A Brief History of Thought: A Philosophical Guide to Living*, trans. Theo Cuffe (New York: HarperCollins, 2011), 52–53. Emphasis original.

that perfectly matched the longings of every heart. "Christianity created a new doctrine of salvation so 'effective' it opened a chasm in the philosophies of Antiquity and dominated the Occidental world for nearly fifteen hundred years."[8]

The second thing to notice is that Paul ties this distinctive hope for the future to the historical, personal resurrection of Jesus: "For since we believe that Jesus died and rose again, even so, through Jesus, God will bring with him those who have fallen asleep" (1 Thess. 4:14). Jesus's resurrection from the dead is both confirmation and model of the resurrection of anyone else who believes. How did Jesus rise again? In a body recognizably his own with his scarred hands and feet, his memories of all he had lived through, and his relationships fully intact.

There are other places in Scripture that point to a personal resurrection, with identities others could recognize and relate to.[9] But the center of this hope is what we see in Christ. His disciples knew him when they saw him. He showed them scars he carried from before his death. They heard his familiar voice. Clearly, he existed on a dimension beyond anything we've ever experienced, with properties his body didn't have before. But he was still Jesus, and those who had known him knew who he was. He rose as himself. So it will be for all those God raises up in the end.

It seems likely Paul wrote this section to encourage Christians who were worried that their lost loved ones would miss out on a future with Jesus when he comes again. These were new Christians,

---

8 Ferry, *Brief History*, 53. See also Everett Ferguson, *Backgrounds of Early Christianity*, 2nd ed. (Grand Rapids, MI: Eerdmans, 1993), 228–34; and Larry Hurtado, *Why on Earth Did Anyone Become a Christian in the First Three Centuries?* (Milwaukee, WI: Marquette University Press, 2016).

9 For further examples, see Randy Alcorn, *Heaven* (Carol Stream, IL: Tyndale House, 2011), 281–82, 345–46.

trusting in a new gospel that was fundamentally different from anything they had heard before. They knew death is a terrible separation. They had always assumed it to be permanent. They were waiting on Christ to come back, just as they'd been taught he would. But then some of them died. Now what? When Jesus comes again, would those loved ones be left behind? Would they be separated from them forever?

Paul wrote these words to comfort them, saying in effect, "Those you love are not finally lost. God will raise them up just as he raised Jesus. You will see them again." This hope is laced through every step in Paul's preview of how things will go when Christ comes again. "The Lord *himself* will descend . . . with a cry of command" (1 Thess. 4:16). The deciding factor is the resurrected voice of Jesus. His cry of command once spoke the world into being. At his cry of command Lazarus staggered out of his tomb. And on the day of his return this same voice will speak a new command, as far-reaching as all the world and as specific as every name graven on his hands and written on his heart, the personal name of every person who died hoping in him. When we hear his voice, those who have died and those who remain alive "will be caught up together." And "we"—as ourselves and knowing one another—"will always be with the Lord" (4:17).

According to the Bible, death is not a basic part of life, a fundamental reality that simply is what it is. We were not born to die after a few brief years of noticing things to cherish before we lose them. We were created to know and to be known, to love and to be loved, then death entered this world as an intruder. It was unleashed on this world as the just consequence of sin. And it exists in this world as our great enemy to be defeated. But when Jesus died and rose again, he won the victory we can't help longing for:

"O death, where is your victory? O death, where is your sting?" (1 Cor. 15:55). Death doesn't win. Love does.

I love how English pastor John Ryland captured Paul's taunting tone at the funeral of his longtime friend in ministry:

> Farewell, thou dear old man! We leave thee in possession of death till the resurrection day: but we will bear witness against thee, oh king of terrors, at the mouth of this dungeon; thou shalt not always have possession of this dead body; it shall be demanded of thee by the great Conqueror, and at that moment thou shalt resign thy prisoner. O ye ministers of Christ, ye people of God, ye surrounding spectators, prepare, prepare to meet this old servant of Christ, at that day, at that hour, when this whole place shall be all nothing, but life and death shall be swallowed up in victory.[10]

We want love after death. And through Christ, in Christ, we will have it.

How to Grieve in Hope

So what about in the meantime? How do we face up to death and what it takes from us while we wait for what Christ has promised? It's crucial, first of all, to accept that grief is not only unavoidable; it's also appropriate for Christians. When Paul says he doesn't want his friends to grieve as those who have no hope he doesn't say he doesn't want them to grieve. He's assuming grief. What matters to him is how they grieve. He wants them to grieve *with hope* and not without it.

---

10 Cited by Peter Naylor, "John Collett Ryland," in *The British Particular Baptists 1638–1910*, vol. 1, ed. Michael Haykin (Springfield, MO: Particular Baptist Press, 1998), 191.

British novelist Julian Barnes, in his memoir *Nothing to Be Frightened Of*, describes the moment when his brother, a fellow atheist, concluded that the claims of Christianity couldn't hold water. It was February 7, 1952. King George VI had just died. The headmaster of his primary school announced that the king "had gone to eternal glory and happiness in heaven with God, and that in consequence we were all going to wear black armbands for a month. I thought there was something fishy there, and how right I was."[11]

Barnes assumed grief and hope are incompatible. If we're wearing black armbands, what does that say about our confidence of eternal glory? If we can't help grieving, our hope must be empty. That is the logic.

But the truth is that Christians have better reasons to grieve freely than anyone else. Let's assume for a moment Barnes's secular perspective on the world. We come from nowhere. We are going nowhere. Any attachment we feel to each other is an evolutionary necessity and nothing more. Death will sever that bond once and for all. It's just simple biology. Why cloak simple biology with sentimentality? What makes what's lost worth grieving over in the first place?

But the backdrop to our hope as Christians is our distinctive view of death and of the grief it causes us. Death is more than simple biology. It is an intruder in God's good world. It is just, but it is unnatural and bound up with sin. Human lives are irreducibly precious. They are designed by God and, in Christ, they are destined for glory. That means the only proper response to every life lost is not resignation but heart-rending, unashamed grief. We are right to grieve over death wherever we see it. We would be wrong not to.

11 Julian Barnes, *Nothing to Be Frightened Of* (New York: Vintage, 2008), 15.

Sometimes with the best of intentions we Christians can fall into our own version of death rebranded as life. When a loved one dies, we say they're in a better place. We hold celebrations of life more often than funerals for the dead. And when we follow this route, sometimes we can even feel guilty for feeling so sad that our loved ones are gone. If they're with Jesus now, why can't I stop crying?

Let me be clear: I do believe those who die in faith are in a better place. And of course, their lives are worth celebrating. But precisely because those loved ones are precious to us, they're worth crying over too. Our ultimate hope is aimed not at where they are now but where we'll be *together* when Christ returns to raise us up.

Our best model for grieving in hope is Jesus himself. In John 11, when he approached the grave of Lazarus, he knew exactly what he was going to do. He had chosen to let his friend die precisely so that he could raise him up again, so that all who saw it might trust him as the resurrection and the life. But when he saw the place where his friend was buried, when he saw the grief of his friends who'd been left behind, Jesus himself wept over Lazarus.

Our grief is not a sign that we don't really believe what we say we believe. It is the Christlike response to the brokenness of a world not made to be this way. Our grief is no denial of hope. It is the backdrop against which hope shines most brightly. We will never see the glory of Christ more clearly than when we look at him through tears.

But here is where we must be careful—to grieve in hope, we must keep our eyes on Christ above all, even as we long to see our friends and families again. We need to know that grief has a powerful role to play in our journey of faith while we wait for the day when he will deliver all that he has promised.

If there is an exception in our culture to the general struggle to connect with heaven, it is in our longing to see friends and family again. For at least the last 150 years, this has been the dominant theme in how American Christians think and talk about heaven. According to historian Gary Smith, "In the middle decades of the nineteenth century, Americans' vision of heaven changed dramatically, from one centered on God to one focused on humans."[12] The most popular books on the subject pictured heaven as an eternal family reunion, with a thick layer of sentimentality that left little room for God as anything more than the keeper of the family home. Andrew Jackson summed up the prevailing idea very well: "Heaven will be no heaven to me if I do not meet my wife there."[13]

I've spent this chapter showing that reunion with those who have died in faith is a bedrock promise of the gospel. It is absolutely worth hoping for. But if when we think of heaven we're thinking first of who we will see again someday, we are missing the point of heaven itself and the purifying purpose of grief in the meantime.

The point of heaven is God. He is its center, its focus, its undisputed main attraction. The psalmist writes, "Whom have I in heaven but you?" (Ps. 73:25). Yes, we will be reunited with one another in his presence. By all means, that happy day is worth longing for. But when we are reunited, we will be united around our joy in seeing him as he is, in living in a world where he is fully and forever with us. What will make our resurrected relationships all the sweeter is the fact that we'll be centered perfectly on him, loving one another for his sake as the God whose goodness gave us our relationships in the first place. Remember what Paul said to the Thessalonians: yes, we will be caught up together. We will be reunited. But the main point is that we, together, will always be with the Lord.

12 Gary Smith, *Heaven in the American Imagination* (New York: Oxford University Press, 2011), 70.
13 Quoted in Smith, *Heaven*, 70.

If we become overly focused on seeing our loved ones again, life in the meantime feels like no more than a holding pattern. It's straight loss, with nothing to do but wait. But grief doesn't have to be a cul-de-sac to wait in while we run out the time we have left. It can be a precious opportunity to taste heaven's joys in advance, with greater sweetness than ever before, because loss can drive us deeper into the love of God. It can be, as C. S. Lewis described it, a "severe mercy."[14] Grief can teach us how good it is to have God for our God.

One of the most treasured books in my library is one my grand-mother gave to me shortly before she died. It's a book by Lewis called *A Grief Observed*, which he wrote to reflect on his own faith after losing his wife to cancer. My grandmother bought the book for help in grieving the death of her youngest son, who died in a car accident driving home from college a few years before I was born. She absolutely devoured this book, marking its pages with underlines and marginal notes, because she wasn't just reading it for interest. She was reading for survival.

One of Lewis's themes she often underlined was how grief over loss tests the quality of your faith—how it exposes what you're trusting in and, even more, shows you what is worth trusting. "You never know how much you really believe anything until its truth or falsehood becomes a matter of life and death to you. . . . Only a real risk tests the reality of a belief."[15] Lewis uses rope as an analogy. It's easy to believe in the quality of a rope that it's strong enough to hold your weight under stress when it's coiled in the box where

14 This phrase comes from a letter by Lewis to his friend Sheldon Vanauken, a relatively new Christian grieving the death of his young wife. Vanauken won a National Book Award for the memoir he wrote about the experience and his friendship with Lewis, *A Severe Mercy* (New York: Harper & Row, 1977).

15 C. S. Lewis, *A Grief Observed* (New York: Bantam, 1976), 25.

you bought it. It's another thing to trust it when you're dangling over the edge of a cliff, hanging on for dear life. Then it becomes crystal clear what your life depends on and whether it can hold your weight. A few pages later, in the margin of Lewis's book, is a penciled note in my grandmother's handwriting: "The rope held me!!! God showed me he is who he said he is!"

I know her grief was excruciating. Of course, she never would have chosen it. But her grief was a refining fire. It drove her deeper into the only refuge there is. For the first thirty-five years of my life, I watched her hold that rope through the declining years of her life, as time took from her more and more of what she loved. I watched her lose basically everything but Jesus, everything but her hold on that rope. But the more she lost, the tighter she held on, and the rope held her still, all the way to the end. As she faced her own death, of course she longed to see her son again. But she also longed to see the one who had held her in her grief, who had become the center of her hope for endless love. She learned through grief that God is who he said he is.

It is through loss that God teaches us to seek first his kingdom, trusting him to add all things in time. Seek God first; restored relationships come later. And while we wait, we learn. We learn how lovely God is in himself, that he is so much more than a means to our ends—even the wonderful end of loving relationships with others. He is the source and the goal for everything good in this world, and he never changes, even as his good gifts come and go.

I began this chapter with a depressing question: What is life after the death of one you love when you don't believe in an afterlife? I'll end it with that same question recast: What is life after the death of one you love when you do believe in an afterlife and grieve in the hope of reunion? The answer is that your life, though changed, is not over. Your grief can serve the greatest purpose in your life. For as long as God gives you breath, you can still do what he made you to do in the first place. You can glorify him and enjoy him, now and forever. You can know from experience what was promised so long ago: "The LORD is near to the brokenhearted" (Ps. 34:18).

7

Bound for Home Together

*How the Hope of Heaven Sets Our
Mission in the Church*

UP TO NOW WE have focused on the many individual benefits of hope to our lives as Christians—on happiness and holiness, on justification and meaning, on peace facing the future, and consolation in the midst of grief. We've focused there because God does; he sets our minds on these good gifts all throughout his word. But the hope of heaven is so much more than individual comfort food, just as heaven itself will be so much more than a pod for my own personal relationship with God.

The biblical vision of the world to come is a corporate vision. Heaven is a kingdom, after all—a realm of perfect peace protected by the perfect justice of the perfect King. It is a city with a culture, a new Jerusalem. And those who will live and love in heaven make up a family, a multiethnic, multinational, and multilingual community of redeemed sinners fused together by mutual devotion to the wonder-working God who made them and made them new.

Every joy of heaven will be enhanced by the joy of sharing it with others, just as a concert or a football game is so much better in the crowd than streamed on your phone. We need to consider how this corporate vision of our future affects our corporate lives in the meantime.

If we stopped short of this corporate dimension, we would not only be missing a crucial aspect of what the Bible says about our future; we would also be guilty of one all-too-common charge against heavenly-mindedness that I mentioned at the very beginning of this book. How can you keep your head in the clouds when there's so much need, so much to be done, all around you? Isn't it self-indulgent to set your mind on an eternal world of bliss when real people are really suffering in *this* world right now?

The perspective of heaven does inform our obligations to those around us in the meantime, both inside and outside the community of believers. Heaven is central to the mission God has given to every local church. And the mission of the local church ought to be central to the life of every individual Christian. In this chapter, I want to share three ways in which the hope of the world to come shapes our mission in the local church—how where we're going defines what we're doing together in the meantime.

We Speak for the Coming King of Heaven

The best place to begin is with the commission Jesus gave to the church just before his ascension to guide our life together until he comes again. The three places where Jesus hands over his mission to his people are wonderfully clear and consistent (Matt. 28:18–20; Luke 24:46–49; Acts 1:8). Each one focuses on transmitting a message from Jesus to the world. Each one relies on the presence of Jesus through the Spirit he will send. Put together, they define the job of the church: speak for the King of heaven, backed by the power of heaven, to invite others to enjoy the kingdom of heaven now and forever.

Consider Acts 1:8, for example: "But you will receive power when the Holy Spirit has come upon you, and you will be my witnesses in Jerusalem and in all Judea and Samaria, and to the end of the earth."[1] Notice the task Jesus gives them: you will be my witnesses, from here to the end of the earth. And notice the power that comes with their mission: the Holy Spirit. Their mission is to proclaim the truth about Jesus, and it will advance as far as the Spirit carries them.

The context of Jesus's statement in Acts is especially helpful for seeing how this simple, straightforward mission connects to the

---

1   Compare Acts 1:8 to the passage known as the Great Commission in Matthew 28:18–20:

> And Jesus came and said to them, "All authority in heaven and on earth has been given to me. Go therefore and make disciples of all nations, baptizing them in the name of the Father and of the Son and of the Holy Spirit, teaching them to observe all that I have commanded you. And behold, I am with you always, to the end of the age."

Notice the emphasis on authority. Jesus is King in heaven and on earth. Now based on his authority he gives a specific job to his people: make disciples of all nations, teaching them to obey his commands. In other words, invite people to embrace Jesus as King. And this commission comes with a promise: Jesus will be with them, empowering them, to the end of the age. In this age, between the time that he leaves the earth and when he comes again, he will be with them as they do what he's told them to do.

In Luke 24:46–49 Jesus uses different words to convey the same basic task backed by the same basic promise:

> [He] said to them, "Thus it is written, that the Christ should suffer and on the third day rise from the dead, and that repentance for the forgiveness of sins should be proclaimed in his name to all nations, beginning from Jerusalem. You are witnesses of these things. And behold, I am sending the promise of my Father upon you. But stay in the city until you are clothed with power from on high."

Jesus tells the disciples that they are witnesses of what he has shown them about himself and of what he wants them to proclaim in his name to all nations: repentance for the forgiveness of sins. For this job they'll be "clothed with power from on high." Their job is to proclaim his message, backed by his power.

beautiful, global promises God has made for our future. In Acts 1:8 Jesus answers the question raised in 1:6, "Lord, will you at this time restore the kingdom to Israel?" This is the right question if you've been well schooled on the prophets. The disciples know God has promised the renewal of his people in the place he prepares for them, where he will be with them, and where perfect peace and justice will reign forever. This world they've been promised is a long way removed from the world they're living in, under the thumb of a cruel and distant emperor. But now they have seen their Master die and come to life again. Luke tells us that Jesus has spent the last forty days speaking to them about the kingdom of God (1:3). Imagine hearing about God's promised future from a resurrected man who is the touchable, visible, quite literal embodiment of that future, breaking into our time and space. Who wouldn't wonder if this was the time for all those promises to come to pass? Who wouldn't long to see heaven on earth then and there?

The reasonable logic behind their question makes Jesus's answer all the more striking and so instructive for us: "It is not for you to know times or seasons that the Father has fixed by his own authority" (1:7). It is not for you to *know times*, much less *to do the work* of establishing heaven on earth. The implications are clear. The Father will enthrone his anointed one. It is God's job to bring about perfect justice, to rid his world of sin, sorrow, pain, and death. But we do have a crucial role with that certain future as our horizon. From now till the end of the age between his comings, Jesus says, "You will be my witnesses" (Acts 1:8). Bear witness to the King and his kingdom. Proclaim the offer of repentance and forgiveness of sin (Luke 24:46–47). Make disciples, and teach them to obey their risen King (Matt. 28:19–20). In other words, Jesus wants them to pass on the message of hope he has given to them, the message he grounded in his death and resurrection.

The words of Jesus frame the mission of the church with both an affirmation and a denial. It *is* our mission to speak for the King of heaven until he comes again so that anyone from anywhere has the chance to enter his kingdom while the gate remains open. It *is not* our mission to build heaven on earth.

This is where many important questions are raised about our responsibility to do good to the societies in which we live, where God in his providence has placed his people. If our mission is to pass on the message of repentance and faith, does that mean Christians don't have to worry about the physical needs we see around us? Do we have nothing to say or do about income inequality, education access, affordable housing, or seeking more just laws overall? Does our focus on heaven and our witness-bearing mission in the meantime imply that we turn a blind eye to the suffering of our neighbors here and now?

Of course not. God has given us so many reasons to care about the vulnerable living around us. For one thing, a crucial part of longing for heaven is longing for the justice that secures heaven's peace. If our hearts belong to a kingdom beyond the oppression, poverty, and suffering so common to our world now, we can't be callous where those conditions exist around us. We can't love heaven rightly without loving the justice that pleases God. And we can't love justice without grieving over injustice where we see it and doing what we can to help in the circumstances where God has placed us.

For another thing, Jesus told us to love our neighbors as we love ourselves. If I want my kids to have access to medical care, I should care whether or not my neighbor's kids have that access too. The same thing goes for food, housing, income, education, and safety under the law, no matter the stage or situation of their lives.

Loving our neighbors as ourselves is part of how we obey all that Jesus commanded us, and it's essential for our lives as his disciples.

The key question for our mission in the church is not whether we want to see our neighbors live lives of physical flourishing. Of course, we should want that for them and seek their flourishing where we can. The key for our mission is how a person comes to experience the blessings of God's kingdom and where God's power is working to expand his kingdom until Christ comes again.

The only way to enter into the blessings of God's kingdom is through repentance and faith. You don't experience those blessings through a hot meal, a better job, or a pro bono legal defense. The gate is narrow. You can only enter on bended knees, with hands that are open to receive forgiveness of sins and the hope of a life beyond this one. If we truly love our neighbors, we won't let anything take our eyes off the witness-bearing mission God has given us.

And where is God's power working to expand his kingdom in this age between Christ's comings? His kingdom expands wherever his Spirit moves—and no further. Where the Holy Spirit is at work, the life of the world to come shows up in our world. What is he doing right now? He is not transforming cities. He is backing the word of the gospel with life-giving power. He is bringing new life to dead hearts, deep love for God's ways, and the rich fruit of faith in the lives of those who believe. He is drawing people into the loving rule of Jesus and building through their life together a preview of the beautiful society of heaven.

We Display the Beautiful Love of Heaven

When the Spirit carries the message of the gospel into hearts made new by his power, the fruit that it bears is love. Jesus himself said that the world would know his disciples by their love for each other, a love that looks like his love for them (John 13:34–35). Paul often made the same connection between God's love for us in Jesus and our love for each other in the church (e.g., Eph. 4:32; Col. 3:12–13). Our model for life together looks backward, in other words, as we live lives shaped by the cross. But our life together looks forward too. In the local church, as the Spirit bears his fruit among us, we're called to offer little previews of the eternal world of love that heaven will be. When we love one another, our words about the King and his kingdom put on flesh.

Perhaps the best place to see the heavenward focus of our love in the church is Paul's beloved description in 1 Corinthians 13. To see the clarity and power of what he says there, we have to rescue his words from the generic and sentimental realm of wall hangings, greeting cards, and wedding invitations. The love Paul celebrates is as concrete and costly as the battered body of Jesus. Paul's purpose is specific too. These beautiful words aimed not to inspire but to correct a self-focused, proud congregation that badly misunderstood where the power of heaven shows up on earth. The Corinthians preferred spiritual gifts you can see, admire, and envy—gifts like tongues, prophecy, or impressive and proprietary knowledge. Paul wrote to convince them that the gift that matters most is love, and to make the case, he tied the *primacy of love* to the *permanency of heaven*:

> Love never ends. As for prophecies, they will pass away; as for tongues, they will cease; as for knowledge, it will pass away. For we know in part and we prophesy in part, but when the perfect comes, the partial will pass away. When I was a child, I spoke like a child, I thought like a child, I reasoned like a child. When I became a man, I gave up childish ways. For now we see in a

mirror dimly, but then face to face. Now I know in part; then I shall know fully, even as I have been fully known.

So now faith, hope, and love abide, these three; but the greatest of these is love. (1 Cor. 13:8–13)

Love matters now because love never ends. Perfect love is our heavenly future. Those who were so caught up with other gifts were obsessing over what won't last and missing the treasure that goes on forever.

That's why Paul goes back to how his own childish ways yielded to maturity. The Corinthians were behaving like kids. Kids overvalue some gifts and vastly undervalue others. Toddlers spend Christmas morning playing with cardboard boxes. Every three-year-old I know would rather have a Ring Pop than a diamond ring. And how many eight-year-olds would choose a Nintendo Switch over Nintendo stock options? Every single one of them.

Paul wants the Corinthians to grow up. They are valuing the wrong gifts for the wrong reasons. They want flashy gifts that boost their status here and now. Paul wants them to treasure what lasts forever. Every other gift is a temporary means to some other end. We won't always need tongues or prophecy. Even faith and hope won't be necessary forever.

Paul doesn't say why love is the greatest of the three great virtues—faith, hope, and love. But I'm convinced by the test that New Testament scholar C. K. Barrett puts to each one.[2]

Does God have faith? No. He doesn't need it. For now, faith is how we cling to our salvation, but one day our faith will be turned to sight.

---

2 C. K. Barrett, *A Commentary on the First Epistle to the Corinthians* (New York: Harper & Row, 1968), 310–11.

Does God have hope? No. He doesn't need hope either. He is the same yesterday, today, and forever. He rules over all and knows exactly what he is doing. For now, we live on hope. So many life-giving promises have yet to be fulfilled. But one day we won't need hope anymore. We will experience for ourselves all that God has prepared for those who love him.

What about love? God doesn't just have love. God is love, in his very being. For now, we see his glory in a mirror dimly. One day we will see him face-to-face. And on the day when he appears, as John put it, "we shall be like him, because we shall see him as he is" (1 John 3:2). When seeing God as he is makes us like him, what will we be like? We will be loving—purely, perfectly loving. Love is the greatest of gifts and the end of them all because God is love, and perfect love is our future.

Perhaps my favorite Christian writing on the world to come is a piece by Jonathan Edwards called "Heaven Is a World of Love," the final chapter of a beloved and accessible book of sermons on 1 Corinthians 13. It's a detailed, thought-provoking, heartwarming catalog of all the ways love will make heaven what it is. Everything there flows from the God at the center of it. God's presence "renders heaven a world of love; for God is the fountain of love, as the sun is the fountain of light. And therefore the glorious presence of God in heaven fills heaven with love, as the sun placed in the midst of the hemisphere in a clear day fills the world with light."[3] The love of God that will capture our hearts is not just beautiful to look at, Edwards argued. It will flow into, out of, and among us. "There the fountain overflows in streams and rivers of love and delight, enough for all to drink at, and to swim in, yea, so as to overflow

---

3 Jonathan Edwards, "Heaven Is a World of Love," in *The Sermons of Jonathan Edwards: A Reader* (New Haven: Yale University Press, 1999), 244–45.

the world as it were with a deluge of love." As God's love moves into and through the saints in heaven, it binds them to each other too and magnifies their delight in being together with him.

> In that soul where divine love reigns, and is in lively exercise, nothing can raise a storm. Those are principles contrary to love which make this world so much like a tempestuous sea. It is selfishness and revenge, and envy, and such things which keep this world in a constant tumult, and make it a scene of confusion and uproar, where no quiet rest is to be enjoyed, unless it be in renouncing the world, and looking to another world. But what rest is there in that world which the God of love and peace fills with his glorious presence, where the Lamb of God lives and reigns, and fills that world with the pleasant beams of his love; where is nothing to give any offense, no object to be seen but what has perfect sweetness and amiableness; where the saints shall find and enjoy all which they love, and so be perfectly satisfied; where there is no enemy and no enmity in any heart, but perfect love in all to everyone; where there is a perfect harmony between the higher and the lower ranks of inhabitants of that world, none envying another, but everyone resting and rejoicing in the happiness of every other.[4]

The best place to see heaven on earth is in the fellowship of a faithful local church, a culture of everyday sacrificial love. If you want to represent God's kingdom in this world, the path forward is not complicated. As Edwards put it, "If you would be in the way to the world of love, you must live a life of love."[5] Join a church,

4   Edwards, "Heaven," 259.
5   Edwards, "Heaven," 271.

with real people marked by limits and flaws, and bear with them. Be patient with the struggling teenager who needs a good friend to disciple him. Be kind to the aging member who needs a ride to church every single week. Rejoice with the woman who has the family you long to have because love does not envy. Speak up when you see a friend embracing what God has condemned when it would be so much easier to say nothing because love does not rejoice in wrongdoing but only in the truth. Believe the best of the frequent stumbler who's trying again to fight for obedience; stand by him over and over again. Organize your life to hold out hope to friends who will sometimes struggle to see it on their own. Love is costly but often uncomplicated. And love is our mission in the church, until Christ comes again. We get to display the beautiful life of heaven until the love of God makes all things new.

We Share the Difficult Journey to Heaven

There is one more way in which the hope of heaven sets our mission in the church. Our hope orients our friendships. The purpose of friendships in the local church is to help each other journey all the way to heaven.

The New Testament consistently speaks of an urgency to our relationships in the church, an urgency that flows from the eternal perspective we gain from the world to come. The book of Hebrews, for example, is laced throughout with the hope of heaven and the need to hold on in faith to the end, building to its famous cast of heroes who model for us the perseverance and perspective we badly need. There is Abraham, who lived as a nomad in the land of promise, "looking forward to the city that has foundations, whose designer and builder is God" (11:10). Or Moses, who chose his people over Pharaoh's house, for "he considered the reproach of

Christ greater wealth than the treasures of Egypt, for he was looking to the reward" (11:26). These and so many more saints of old lived and died with their hearts set on God's promised future:

> These all died in faith, not having received the things promised, but having seen them and greeted them from afar, and having acknowledged that they were strangers and exiles on the earth. For people who speak thus make it clear that they are seeking a homeland. If they had been thinking of that land from which they had gone out, they would have had opportunity to return. But as it is, they desire a better country, that is, a heavenly one. Therefore God is not ashamed to be called their God, for he has prepared for them a city. (Heb. 11:13–16)

This future-oriented faith defines the Christian life too. We're called to live as strangers and exiles for now—not because this world has nothing to recommend it but because we desire a better country, a true and lasting homeland. We live our lives on a journey just as they did.

It is dangerous, even impossible, to face this journey alone. That's why, before giving these positive models of Old Testament faith, the author of Hebrews warns us of what happened to Israel in the wilderness and calls us to make sure no one else falls as they did: "Take care, brothers, lest there be in any of you an evil, unbelieving heart, leading you to fall away from the living God. But exhort one another every day, as long as it is called 'today,' that none of you may be hardened by the deceitfulness of sin" (3:12–13). The writer assumes we are vulnerable to deception and unbelief. But he also assumes we will know that about one another, pay attention to each other's lives, and be willing to guard each other against threats we may not see by ourselves. There is a whole world of hard conversations built into those simple verses. It would be so much easier to pass the time talking about baseball than flagging danger, confronting sin, or facing up to someone else's probing questions. But if we see one another as pilgrims together in a dangerous time, trudging through our wilderness like Israel before us, vulnerable on our own just as they were, we won't be able to live with what silence might mean for the ones we love.

It is also the hope of heaven that gathers us week after week. Hebrews 10 places the day of Christ's return at the backdrop of every single church service: "And let us consider how to stir up one another to love and good works, not neglecting to meet together, as is the habit of some, but encouraging one another, and all the more as you see the Day drawing near" (10:24–25). Sunday after Sunday, we show up to encourage one another. We don't stop because we know we can't live without that encouragement, just as our friends need to get it from us. In every single gathering, we are singing and praying and reading and preaching one another one week closer to the day that is drawing near.

For any of us to make it to heaven, we need friends to keep our eyes on the promise and to guard our hearts against any alternative in the meantime. That's what a local church is for. It is simply a group of Christian friends who promise to help each other follow Jesus from here to glory.

I think my favorite character in John Bunyan's *Pilgrim's Progress* is not Christian, the main protagonist, but Hopeful, his steady companion. Bunyan's allegory of the Christian life follows the twists and turns of Christian's journey, from his conversion in the City of Destruction to his home in heaven, the Celestial City. Christian is the one whose steps we're meant to follow, but Hopeful is beside him on the way, reminding him of the truth of the gospel, building him up when his spirits are low, warning him when he's tempted, holding him up when he's weak, and keeping his eyes always on where they're going.

My favorite scene is when the pair has finally reached the gates of the Celestial City, separated only by the rushing river that represents death. On the banks of this river, Christian is overwhelmed by doubt. As soon as they step into the water, he goes down. His feet can't feel the bottom. He's bobbing up and down, gasping for air. He's utterly convinced that he won't be able to reach the other side. But just as he is losing his grip on hope, Hopeful is there, right next to him, guiding him all the way through. He assures Christian that he can feel the bottom though Christian cannot. He reminds Christian of the promises he is struggling to remember. And he tells Christian what he can see of their destination, until once again Christian sees it for himself. Hopeful's friendship carries Christian through the river and all the way home.[6]

That is our mission in each other's lives. Our goal in the church is to help each other make it across the river as we face whatever confronts us along the way. Can you see what the perspective of heaven does to the consumerism that so often cripples local churches in America? In our church's class for new members, I often compare what it is to board a cruise ship to what it is to join a crew team. If you're thinking about boarding a cruise ship, you're evaluating various benefits and services, doing your best to get the most bang for your buck. Is there a well-credentialed chef, and what are the options on each menu? How large are the rooms, how soft are the beds, and how many swimming pools are

6   John Bunyan, *The Pilgrim's Progress*, ed. W. R. Owens (1678; repr., New York: Oxford University Press, 2003), 147–48.

onboard? What are the entertainment options during the voyage, and will the ship be stopping in cities I want to visit? Your focus is on what you hope to get and whether the benefits outweigh the costs.

With a crew team everything is different. What matters are your responsibilities, not your amenities. You'll have an oar in your hands. This boat will rely on the strength of your back to get where it is going. Your team will depend on you as you depend on them. What matters most is where you are headed and how you will help each other get there.

In the consumeristic, choice-saturated culture where we live, it is all too easy for us to approach our churches as if they were cruise ships. We scrutinize the services and amenities, and even after boarding we can stay in evaluation mode, in case another ship comes along offering a better fit for a better price. We can turn our churches into yet another venue for living our best lives now.

The perspective of heaven is a precious gift to guard us against such worldliness. When we see our churches for where we're headed and why we're needed, we will know better. We're not here for the amenities. We're here on the mission given to us by the King who died and rose for us. Who cares whether the band plays our favorite songs in just the way we like them? Who cares whether there's a climbing wall for our kids in the youth wing? Who cares whether we're getting as much as we're giving in our relationships? We're not here to live our best lives now. We're here to represent Jesus to each other and to make sure our friends make it across the river.

I don't know of a better text for perspective on the life of the local church than the prophecy of Isaiah 25:6–8. It begins as a picture of heaven and ends as a conversation among friends.

On this mountain the LORD of hosts will make for all peoples
    a feast of rich food, a feast of well-aged wine,
    of rich food full of marrow, of aged wine well refined.
And he will swallow up on this mountain
    the covering that is cast over all peoples,
    the veil that is spread over all nations.
    He will swallow up death forever;
and the Lord GOD will wipe away tears from all faces,
    and the reproach of his people he will take away from all
        the earth,
    for the LORD has spoken.

The world to come is like a party fully stocked and never ending, where death itself is swallowed up in the feast. There will be no more tears because God will wipe them away himself, and there will be no more reason for crying again. It's the prophecy behind the beautiful language of Revelation 21, at the center of our hope for a better world.

But look how Isaiah's image of heaven concludes:

It will be said on that day,
    "Behold, this is our God; we have waited for him, that he
        might save us.
    This is the LORD; we have waited for him;
    let us be glad and rejoice in his salvation." (Isa. 25:9)

It concludes with a conversation among friends who have waited together. *We* have waited for him. Let *us* be glad and rejoice in his salvation. This day of celebration will be irreducibly communal because our hope in the meantime is communal too.

When I imagine the conversation of Isaiah 25, I think of specific people with whom I've shared life in my church. I think of my friend Eric, a dear and faithful brother who trusted the Lord through years of excruciating pain that made it impossible for him to work.

I think of Ms. Sue, who joined our church in the 1950s. She taught Sunday school for decades, discipled generations of women, and kept showing up amid a pandemic, pulling her oxygen tank behind her, because she saw the day drawing near.

I think of Mitchell and Amanda, who chose to have their first baby in a Central Asian city thousands of miles from their families and friends, hoping to share heaven's joys with people whose names they don't yet know.

I think of single friends who have waited on the Lord in their longing for a family. Of brothers in the fight against porn they love and hate—falling, rising, and fighting on in the hope of perfect holiness to come. Of friends who have suffered inexplicable depression and anxiety, who hate the way they feel but have forged ahead under the clouds, watching, praying, and longing for the day when there will be no more sorrow or pain.

I think of my church's membership directory, where every smiling face belongs to a personal story of sin and salvation, of joy and sorrow, of suffering, hope, and groaning for the world to come. And as we share our life together now, I'm thinking of the day when he will return, and we will say to each other, with knowing looks and hearts full of joy, "This is the Lord! We have waited for him together, and he's here! Let us be glad and rejoice in his salvation."

Our mission in the church is to hold out the hope of that day so that we can share in its joy with a multitude from every tribe and tongue and nation. It is this hope that sets our mission in the meantime.

Conclusion

On Things Above

*Why Our Longing for More Makes
All the Sense in the World*

MY GOAL HAS BEEN TO SHOW the everyday benefit of what you might call a cultivated heavenly-mindedness. Even those of us who affirm the Bible's teaching about the world to come often have trouble seeing the relevance of *that world* to *this world*. Chapter by chapter, I've tried to show the wonderful usefulness of hope in heaven for life in the meantime to urge you toward an active focus on all that God has promised for your future.

All that said, C. S. Lewis's challenge to critics of heaven in his day is worth posing to ourselves too: the primary question is not whether heaven is useful to life on earth but whether the promise of heaven is true in the first place. If there is no heaven, "then Christianity is false, for this doctrine is woven into its whole fabric. If there is, then this truth, like any other, must be faced, whether it is useful at political meetings or no."[1] Lewis is exactly right. Whether

---

1 C. S. Lewis, *The Problem of Pain* (New York: Collier, 1962), 144–45.

focus on heaven is pie-in-the-sky escapism or life-shaping practical realism comes down to whether or not heaven truly exists. So, does it? How could we know? And what difference does it make to the Christian life?

The Challenge of Our Longing

I first encountered Ludwig Feuerbach, the nineteenth-century German thinker, in my first semester of graduate school. Our professor assigned *The Essence of Christianity* to show us how philosophers began to treat Christianity the way the Bible treats pagan religion. Isaiah famously mocks the idol craftsman for his do-it-yourself approach to the divine. He cuts a tree, he measures its wood, he bakes his bread over a fire made of one half, then bows and worships an idol he carves from the other (Isa. 44:12–17). For Feuerbach and his ilk, Christianity is no less man made and all rooted in the longings of the human heart.

He believed that we project our desires onto a being that we call God and into a new world that we call heaven. We want justice, so we project a God who can establish what justice is and punish those who don't comply. We want forgiveness, so we project a God of mercy and compassion who makes a way for sinners to be restored. We want protection and provision in a world full of threats and uncertainty, so we project a God who is powerful and paying attention to us. And at the most fundamental level, at the essential core of what religion is all about, we want to live beyond the reach of death. So, we project an eternal God who shares his eternal home with us.

For Feuerbach, God is *how* we get what we want, heaven is *where* we will get what we want, and both depend on us for their existence. He writes,

The belief in heaven, or in a future life in general, rests on a mental judgment. It expresses praise and blame. . . . That which man thinks beautiful, good, agreeable, is for him what alone ought to be; that which he thinks bad, odious, disagreeable, is what ought not to be . . . the other world is nothing more than the reality of a known idea, the satisfaction of a conscious desire, the fulfillment of a wish.[2]

The pagans made their gods out of a piece of wood. Christians make their God out of a longing heart.

Feuerbach was one of the first and most influential purveyors of what you might call cultivated hopelessness. Our hunger for something more, for a world beyond the limits of this one, deceives us at best. At worst it deprives us of what might be had here and now. Better to do combat against the deepest longings of the human heart.

From what I can see, this way of thinking has been wildly successful at spreading hopelessness in our secular age, but it has done nothing at all to ease our hunger for more than what we see and experience in this world as it is. Just consider a few of the most obvious ways our culture is distinct from other times and places.

Our devotion to distraction. Nearly seven million viewers took in the *Golden Bachelor* finale. By my count, there have been six installments so far in the *Sharknado* film franchise. Streaming services have stopped even asking if you want to play the next episode of whatever series you're into. And all this is to say nothing of what we're watching, reading, communicating, or playing on our phones in an average day. What should we make of all this distraction?

2   Ludwig Feuerbach, *The Essence of Christianity*, trans. George Eliot (1841; repr., Amherst, NY: Prometheus Books, 1989), 177–78.

What does it say of us as a culture that we've consumed forty-six seasons of *Survivor* and counting? Certainly not that we're loving life. No one wants to be distracted from their overwhelming happiness. More likely there's something we would rather not face up to. We look like a culture desperate to escape our reality, one episode at a time. We try to quiet our longings through amusement and distraction, but it isn't working.

Our exhausting obsession with work. Right alongside our culture's penchant for distraction, the problem of burnout is on a startling rise in America, especially among younger generations. Whatever else may contribute to this trend, at the very least it shows a longing to do something meaningful with your life. But what would it even look like to accomplish something meaningful in a world where your own descendants won't remember you one hundred years after your death? Remember how philosopher Thomas Nagel put it: "Even if you produce a great work of literature which continues to be read thousands of years from now, eventually the solar system will cool or the universe will wind down or collapse, and all trace of your efforts will vanish."[3] It's little wonder the novelist John Updike explained his prolific output by the sense that his work was like riding a bicycle. You have to keep on pedaling as hard as you can because you'll only go as far as you can push yourself. And as soon as you stop you will crash.[4] We try to fulfill our longings through *more* meaningful, *more* successful, and *more* enviable work at whatever matters to us. But it isn't working.

Our relentless personal consumption. Perhaps nothing better captures the distinctiveness of our secular age than our insatiable

3   Thomas Nagel, *What Does It All Mean?: A Very Short Introduction to Philosophy* (New York: Oxford University Press, 1987), 96.
4   John Updike, *Self-Consciousness* (New York: Knopf, 1985), 228.

drive to get more. It's not contentment that makes the modern world go round. It's craving. There's a reason we browse "best-of" tech buyer's guides every year before Christmas. What if the "best" bluetooth speaker of October 2024 is better than the "best" speaker I bought this time last year? In 1930, the average American woman had nine outfits. As of a few years ago, the average number was thirty. In 2015, the average American family spent $1,700 on clothes, throwing out something like sixty-five pounds of clothes per year.[5] And what child ever bought a set of LEGOs and thought, "Now my collection is complete"? Have you ever felt like you have enough? We try to redirect our longings for something transcendent toward objects we can purchase and own here and now, but this isn't working either.

Our secular age is certainly less hopeful, but the signs are so very clear: we are no less hungry than ever. Hopelessness has done nothing to relieve our longing for more.

The Clue in Our Longing

What if instead of suppressing our longings or redirecting them in one way after another, we chose to listen to them and to learn from them?

One of the most distinctive things about us humans is the resilience of our longing for more life in a better world. We crave justice and are bothered by injustice (especially against ourselves) in a way that the mockingbirds nesting in my yard don't seem to be. We are hungry for meaning—meaningful work, meaningful relationships, meaningful legacies, and so much more. I've never noticed that hunger in my son's bearded dragon. He seems satisfied with a UV

---

5   Emma Johnson, "The Real Cost of Your Shopping Habits," *Forbes*, January 15, 2015, https://www.forbes.com/.

light and a steady supply of crickets. Have you ever wondered why humans struggle so much to accept the reality of death and what that means for life in the world? It's as basic to human experience as birth, eating, and sleeping. It's the fate we share with all creatures, from kitty cats to cockroaches. The author of Ecclesiastes agonizes over sharing such fate with the beasts.

> For what happens to the children of man and what happens to the beasts is the same; as one dies, so dies the other. They all have the same breath, and man has no advantage over the beasts, for all is vanity. All go to one place. All are from the dust, and to dust all return. Who knows whether the spirit of man goes upward and the spirit of the beast goes down into the earth? (Eccl. 3:19–21)

No dog that I know of has ever had this complaint. Why is that? Feuerbach saw our longings as evidence *against* the possibility of heaven. The essence of Christianity is wishful thinking. Because we long for a world beyond the reach of death and all its minions, such a world must not exist. We invent heaven to help ourselves sleep through the night. But what if the truth is the other way around?

Lewis saw our longings as evidence *for* the existence of something we long to see. How did we get these longings in the first place? How could a blind and empty cosmos give birth to desires so much greater than itself? Does it not make more sense to believe that longings like ours are a sign of our true condition?

> Creatures are not born with desires unless satisfaction for those desires exists. A baby feels hunger: well, there is such a thing as food. A duckling wants to swim: well, there is such a thing as

water. Men feel sexual desire: well, there is such a thing as sex. If I find in myself a desire which no experience in this world can satisfy, the most probable explanation is that I was made for another world.[6]

Now admittedly, the sheer fact of our longing for more is at most a clue to the possibility of a world beyond what we see and know now. It's worth taking seriously, but it can't confirm a distinctly Christian account of the world to come. This desire for connection to something beyond ourselves explains why there are pyramids in Egypt, a circle of pillars at Stonehenge, and ruined temples on every acropolis in Greece. But why should we believe that *heaven* is what we're longing for, much less that it's really there to be enjoyed?

The Confirmation of Our Longing

There is one fundamental reason to believe that the better world of the Bible's promises is not just a world that we are longing for but a world that's sure to come. We know we can live in bodies beyond the reach of death because Jesus already has one. Everything rests on the historical, physical resurrection of Jesus. In 1 Corinthians 15 Paul treats the resurrection of Jesus as stunning and unexpected. That's why he lists witnesses to confirm that it really happened. He won't settle for wishful thinking. He writes, "If in Christ we have hope in this life only, we are of all people most to be pitied" (1 Cor. 15:19). A merely therapeutic benefit, a jolt of optimism and positivity—that isn't enough for Paul, and it shouldn't be enough for us either. Any hope confined to the breath that is this life is simply pitiful. That is not the sort of hope we have:

---

6   C. S. Lewis, *Mere Christianity* (1952; repr., New York: HarperCollins, 2001), 136–37.

But in fact Christ has been raised from the dead, the firstfruits of those who have fallen asleep. . . . For as in Adam all die, so also in Christ shall all be made alive. But each in his own order: Christ the firstfruits, then at his coming those who belong to Christ. (1 Cor. 15:20, 22–23)

Paul sees the resurrection of Jesus as the first step in an organic process that is unified and unstoppable. Jesus's resurrection isn't just about Jesus. When he walked out of the grave where he was laid, his new body broke through the ground as the firstfruits of a harvest that's coming. His resurrection implies the resurrection of everyone who trusts in him, and his present life is a living and breathing preview of our certain future.

Because It Is True

If the resurrection of Jesus belongs at the center of our hope as Christians, it also places longing for heaven at the center of our lives. Heavenly-mindedness isn't an escape from the troubles we'd rather not think about. It isn't dodging responsibilities we'd rather not have or a sign we don't care about the suffering of our neighbors. It doesn't mean that we're sick of life on earth or that we have no love for this world as it is. And it isn't only for elderly saints in hospice care. Heavenly-mindedness is basic Christianity. It is the only reasonable response to the fact of Jesus's resurrection from the dead and the sign that we believe it's really true. It is the living conviction that Christ is risen and soon returning.

Over and over again, Paul describes the Christian life as a life of waiting because we expect to get what Christ already has: "Our citizenship is in heaven, and from it we await a Savior, the Lord Jesus Christ, who will transform our lowly body to be like his glorious body, by the power that enables him even to subject all things to himself" (Phil. 3:20–21; cf. Rom. 8:23–25; 1 Cor. 1:7; Gal. 5:5; 1 Thess. 1:10; Titus 2:13). But the waiting he's calling for is not the mind-numbing, thumb-twiddling, time-wasting plight of a line at the DMV or Passport Control. It's more like the way I wait in line at my favorite local burrito shop. I'm feeling the rumble in my stomach. I'm locked in on the menu that I'll choose from. And I'm watching the front of the line—every customer who walks away with food is confirmation that my feast is coming soon. This sort of waiting is crisp, focused, and active.

In Paul's life as a Christian, the best synonym for waiting is groaning:

> For while we are still in this tent, we *groan*, being burdened— not that we would be unclothed, but that we would be further clothed, so that what is mortal may be swallowed up by life. He who has prepared us for this very thing is God, who has given us the Spirit as a guarantee. (2 Cor. 5:4–5)

> . . . but we ourselves, who have the firstfruits of the Spirit, *groan* inwardly as we wait eagerly for adoption as sons, the redemption of our bodies. (Rom. 8:23)

Paul connects the groaning of our hearts to the work of God's Spirit in us. Groaning for heaven is spiritual maturity. It is the sign that God's Spirit is growing faith in God's word about God's Son.

Is this groaning a priority for your growth as a Christian? My goal in this book has been to convince you that it ought to be and, even more, to help you deepen that groaning day by day. If longing for heaven is crucial for growth, heavenly-mindedness is how we feed it. We use our minds to warm our hearts toward all that God has promised for our future. This is the work of faith for as long as Jesus tarries. And as we do this work, we should pray as Baxter prayed: "Help me desire until I may possess."[7]

---

7   Richard Baxter, *The Saints' Everlasting Rest*, updated and abridged by Tim Cooper (Wheaton, IL: Crossway, 2022), 155.

General Index

Abraham, 133
Adam, 8, 23–24
Afterlife (Gervais), 105–6
Allen, Michael, 15n11
anxiety, 73–74
  and the pressure of responsibility, 85–86
  as a warning sign, 85
  See also anxiety, understanding of
anxiety, understanding of, 74–75
  knowing our future is up to us, 76–78
  knowing our future is vulnerable, 75–76
Augustine, 21

Baldwin, James, 14
Barnes, Julian, 116
Barrett, C. K., 130
Baxter, Richard, 8–9, 10, 11, 65–66
  on keeping our memory of earth while in heaven, 102
Bible, the, 63, 85
  biblical vision of the world to come, 123–24
  on death, 114–15
  description of heaven in, 5, 13
  expressions of hope in, 23
  on redemption and salvation, 15n11

Brief History of Thought, A (Ferry), 112
Bruised Reed, The (Sibbes), 72
burnout, problem of, 45

Chalmers, Thomas, 67
Christianity, 110, 113, 114, 116, 141, 142, 146, 148
Christian life, the, 148–49
  focus on heaven, 3
  foundation of, 13
Christians, 113–14, 115
  American Christians' view of heaven, 118
  benefits of hope to Christians, 123
  and the day of judgment, 46–47
  and hope, 116
  on thinking about heaven, 4
church, the
  goal of, 136–37
  mission of, 127–28
consumption, personal, 144–45
culture
  consumer culture, 137
  Western culture, 77

David, 23, 27, 28, 31–32
Davis, Chris, 48–49
day of judgment, 46–49, 48n8
  remembering of, 54–56

Scripture Index

TGC THE GOSPEL COALITION

The Gospel Coalition (TGC) supports the church in making disciples of all nations, by providing gospel-centered resources that are trusted and timely, winsome and wise.

Guided by a Council of more than 40 pastors in the Reformed tradition, TGC seeks to advance gospel-centered ministry for the next generation by producing content (including articles, podcasts, videos, courses, and books) and convening leaders (including conferences, virtual events, training, and regional chapters).

In all of this we want to help Christians around the world better grasp the gospel of Jesus Christ and apply it to all of life in the 21st century. We want to offer biblical truth in an era of great confusion. We want to offer gospel-centered hope for the searching.

Join us by visiting TGC.org so you can be equipped to love God with all your heart, soul, mind, and strength, and to love your neighbor as yourself.

TGC.org

Also Available from
Matthew McCullough

Claiming that the best way to find meaning in life is to get honest about death, this book aims to show readers the practical effect of remembering their mortality in order to make the most of their lives today.

For more information, visit **crossway.org**.